# THE
# Old Rittenhouse Inn
# COOKBOOK

## Meals & Memories from the
## Historic Bayfield B&B

by Mark Phillips

Lake Superior
Port Cities Inc.

First Edition: July 2014

Lake Superior Port Cities Inc.
P.O. Box 16417
Duluth, Minnesota 55816-0417 USA
888-BIG LAKE (888-244-5253)

5 4 3 2 1

Library of Congress Cataloging-in-Publication Data

Phillips, Mark, 1971-
    The Old Rittenhouse Inn cookbook : meals & memories of the historic Bayfield
B&B / Mark Phillips. – First edition.
        pages cm
    Includes index.
    ISBN 978-1-938229-19-0
    1. Cooking, American. 2. Old Rittenhouse Inn. 3. Cooking – Wisconsin –
Bayfield County. 4. Bayfield County (Wis.) – Social life and customs. I. Title.
    TX715.P568 2014
    641.5973 – dc23                                    2014014826

Editors: Konnie LeMay, Ann Possis, Barb LeMasurier, Cindy Marshall Hayden
Design: Tanya Bäck

Cover images: Mark Phillips (Old Rittenhouse Inn), Christian Giannelli (Crab Cakes)
Inside images: Most photos are from the Old Rittenhouse Inn or are courtesy of the
Bayfield Chamber & Visitor Bureau. Food photos mainly are by Christian Giannelli.
Printer: Friesens, printed in Canada

To my children, Kyra June Phillips and Max Daniel Phillips,
and to all the generations who stayed here and worked here,
past, present and future, sharing our dreams and making them come to life.

# Acknowledgments

Though my name is on the cover, this book belongs to all of us here at the Inn: the Phillips family and our extended family of employees.

Of course this is Mary and Jerry Phillips' story. It was their dream to start with, and it has been shared by so many over the years. Wendy and I are carrying the dream on now, so it is our book as well.

For many of our guests, Julie Phillips is the face of the Inn, the person with whom they have the most contact during their stay. They might try one of her signature cocktails or a special wine she suggested. Julie might serve their breakfast. And she's sure to offer insider advice about what to do while you're in town. So this is her story, too.

This is also Matt Chingo's book, and it couldn't have been completed without him. The executive chef at Old Rittenhouse Inn since 2012, and sous chef before that, Matt is a true leader in our kitchen. With his beautiful plates, delicious food and positive work ethic, he sets a great example for our kitchen team. Despite a busy schedule, Matt wrote out each recipe I requested, long after I'd promised that we were "done adding recipes." He always has a pleasant attitude. I can't thank him enough.

We thank the others who have served as our head chefs since Mary's retirement in 1992: Larry Cicero, Bill Rohling, Mark Wolslegel, David Miller and Steven Keen.

Here on the porch are our two generations of the Phillips family's Old Rittenhouse Innkeepers – me (Mark), Wendy, Jerry and Mary. On the facing page, Mom and Dad (Mary and Jerry) sit in the Inn's dining room circa 1995.

*Hilary Cronon*

The book is also for all the other employees: the maintenance, housekeeping, dishwashers and prep cooks, groundskeepers, hosts and wait staff. These people all work to keep the Inn looking beautiful and running smoothly. Often they work behind the scenes. They are the unsung heroes of the Inn.

We'd also like to thank Paul and Cindy Hayden, Konnie LeMay and the entire team at Lake Superior Port Cities Inc., whose ongoing efforts to promote Lake Superior and the North Woods via print and digital media are absolutely vital to our region. This "labor of love" you now hold in your hands would not be possible without their talents, support and guidance.

This book also belongs in part to my grandmothers, June Stuessy and Margaret Phillips. The former raised an exceptional only child. The latter raised 10 children. Both were farm wives. Each was an amazing cook who loved the growing, the harvesting, the preparation and the ultimate enjoyment and nourishment of the foods that they raised. Love went into their cooking, always.

Even before she joined our family as my wife, Wendy has been part of our story. She worked here as a young woman and today is the backbone of the Inn, smoothing the daily operations while preserving the magical experience for each guest. She is the bedrock of our family, too, and, along with our children, is the love of my life.

Most of all this book belongs to my mother, Mary, without whom none of it would be possible. Her dream carried us to today's success. It's a dream in which we still believe.

# Contents

# Welcome to Our Home,
# Welcome to Our Table

Dear Reader,

Before we begin this journey, before we get to the recipes, stories and photographs from 40 years of the Old Rittenhouse Inn and Landmark Restaurant, I'd like to take a moment to introduce you to my family and to tell you why I wrote this book.

The innkeeping Phillips family consists of me (Mark) and my wife (Wendy), my parents (Jerry and Mary, who started the Old Rittenhouse Inn), and my aunt (Jerry's sister Julie). The next generation is our children (Kyra and Max).

Our family has been innkeeping since 1975, providing an experience of Victorian lodging and fine dining with an absence of pretension. We have had hundreds of thousands of guests for overnight stays, and also for breakfast, brunch, lunch or dinner. Over the years, there's been a wonderful collaboration between our chefs developing recipes and our guests refining those choices by indicating their favorites. Some of these recipes we use every day, others we save for special occasions, but each recipe in this book has stood the test of time.

We chose recipes based on three main factors: The main ingredient(s) are locally raised or harvested; the recipe is a "signature" dish served frequently at Landmark or often requested by guests; the dish is a classic, something from our first cookbook, *Favorite Recipes from the Old Rittenhouse Inn*, developed by our original chef and owner/innkeeper, Mary Phillips.

But food alone does not make a life. Along with the recipes, I've included a few stories from our family's time at the Inn and lots of photographs, not just of food and our Inn, but of our family and community – all the things that have influenced the evolution of Old Rittenhouse Inn and made richer experiences for our guests.

In a manner of speaking, I have been an "innkeeper" since I was 4 years old. That was my age in 1975 when Dad and Mom rented a large U-Haul truck, packed up our belongings with the help of friends and left our house in Oregon, Wisconsin, for the northern edge of the state. I must have slept most of the way north because the next thing I knew we were pulling into Bayfield, coasting down Rittenhouse Avenue and waiting for the first glimpse of our "Northern Castle," as I called it. There it was: The big red house on the hill. As you read about our stories through my eyes, you'll find that I sometimes refer to "Mom and Dad" or "Mary and Jerry." That's one of the quirks of growing up so publicly and of sharing my folks with all of our guests.

Over the years, watching my parents at work and meeting others in the business, I have come to some conclusions about innkeepers. Most have big hearts. We share a love and respect for our historic buildings, for our employees and for our guests, who become our extended family. Nothing makes our day more than to hear a guest say that someone on our staff made their stay "over the top," "spectacular" or "the best ever."

Just like our Inn, a lot of love went into this book. A house becomes a home by what goes on inside it. A cookbook, too, is more than a collection of ingredients and instructions. It is a collection of memories because the most meaningful moments in life often are spent with our family and friends around a table.

So many flavors bring to my mind images of family: Aunt Julie's spinach dip, my dad's pot roast, my grandmother's cherry pie. Our family get-togethers would not be the same without those favorite dishes, and they still evoke fond memories even after family members are no longer with us at the table. At the Inn's Landmark Restaurant, we also create memories with special dishes and meals served here would not be the same without the recipes we've included on these pages.

In this book, you'll read about some of the trials and tribulations of growing a country inn bed and breakfast business from its infancy – and more or less from my infancy. I was privileged to "grow up B&B," to have a houseful of moms and dads, and to learn about the magic of opening your doors to guests, familiar and new.

This book touches on the things grown and cultivated in our region and the people who work the land and fish the inland sea. It will introduce Lake Superior and our north woods and a few of our celebrations. Mainly, though, this is about family and about food.

As you read about my family and my life, please consider your own life's memories and how food weaves through them. Sometimes a memory, like a casual snapshot, becomes more meaningful over time. This book is composed of our favorite dishes, returned to time and again, and of memories gathered from a lifetime of innkeeping.

If you have been an overnight guest at Old Rittenhouse Inn, or if you have enjoyed dinner at Landmark, I hope you will enjoy this book and will recall your own special memories. If you have yet to join us at the Inn, please read on. Savor the recipes, photos and stories and perhaps we can persuade you to make a visit to our fantastic town.

May your life be filled with good food, good friends … and always a good night's stay.

Mark Phillips, Innkeeper, 2014
Old Rittenhouse Inn

# Our Beginnings

## It All Starts with Falling In Love …

For my parents, Mary and Jerry Phillips, the couple who created Old Rittenhouse Inn, everything seems to start with falling in love.

First, they fell in love with each other as students at the University of Wisconsin-Madison. He sang in the Glee Club and the Wisconsin Singers, and she was the piano accompanist (and thus the only woman in the all-male Glee Club). "I just admired her so much. I loved her music," Jerry says, adding, however, that the feeling apparently was not mutual. Mary first avoided him, going so far as to turn a different direction when she saw him. She pegged him for a "frat boy" (which he was not, Jerry notes).

One day Jerry needed help to practice a difficult piece of music – "Ave Maria" – he was to perform for a wedding. He asked a friend to find a pianist. Until he walked into the room that day to meet his pianist, Jerry didn't know it was Mary. She definitely did not know it would be Jerry. She froze with a glare that bore into him. Jerry blurted out, "I can't believe it! This is the best luck ever to have the best person in the world to play for me." Apparently it was the right thing to say; they pretty much have stayed together since.

Next Mary and Jerry fell in love with a small town and a Great Lake. A honeymoon side trip brought them to Bayfield, Wisconsin, in 1969. They instantly adored this sleepy little fishing town that back then was yet to be rediscovered.

"I'll never forget our first sight of Bayfield," Jerry recalls. "It was a sunny, warm day in June. We were mesmerized by the lake sparkling like a million diamonds. We were completely spellbound."

Bayfield, on a hillside overlooking Lake Superior, had gone through a series of booms and busts since its founding in 1856. By the time the 1970s (and the Phillips) arrived, the city's historic buildings had been "preserved by neglect," as Jerry is fond of saying. A

*Christian Giannelli*

A "Superior" view from Le Château's front porch.

lack of fix-up money kept the historic architecture of Bayfield from being modernized – just what they wanted.

Finally, Mary and Jerry fell in love with a building. The great big red Victorian mansion seemed to be waiting for them on the corner of Rittenhouse Avenue and Third Street. Its massive wrap-around front porch was punctuated with pillars on blocks of locally quarried brownstone. It had multiple gables and numerous windows facing out over the town of Bayfield and Lake Superior. It was destined to be theirs, though they didn't know it in 1969.

# Wedding Bells

When Jerry decided to propose to Mary, he did the proper thing and asked permission of Mary's mother, an amazing woman he admired very much.

"I'd really like to marry your daughter," Jerry told her mom, "but if you wouldn't consent to that, could I at least marry you?"

She consented to the former offer and was amused by the latter. Mary and Jerry selected the church based on who had the best pipe organ in town.

"Then we organized a concert for before the ceremony with all our favorite singers and instrumentalists from Madison. We sneaked into the sacristy together to listen."

Mary has always been strong and brave. As her father was deceased, Jerry asked who she wanted to bring her down the aisle at their wedding.

"No one," she replied without pause. "I want to come to you by myself."

"I will never forget watching Mary as she came up that long center aisle, all alone, so strong, so radiant," Jerry recalls. "My eyes filled with tears and my heart, well, it's still overflowing."

# Jumping Inn

The world moves in mysterious ways, certainly in the lives of the Phillips family.

After university, Jerry and Mary found work as music teachers and musicians. She worked in junior high school and loved the roller-coaster enthusiasms of that age group. For a time, Jerry directed the Madison Savoyards, a troupe that performs Gilbert & Sullivan plays. He also taught music at junior and senior high schools and in a seminary. They worked as a team doing the music program for a Madison church.

When they came to Bayfield on that 1969 honeymoon trip, they were just escaping the drenching rains that day in Hayward, where they were staying. The sun shone in Bayfield and the city was (and is) beautiful. Mary and Jerry drove the streets, exclaiming about historic house after house. They loved how the steep hills gave everyone a view.

Then they saw an incredible house with fountains and grapevines. Le Château, as they would come to call the Boutin mansion, was overgrown and somewhat neglected, but nevertheless the property was amazing. A big sign out front read "Mose Theno Realty." Back then, Bayfield was near the bottom of a deep economic downturn. There were vacant buildings and "For Sale" signs everywhere. Buildings were selling low.

But back in Oregon, a small town south of Madison, Mary and Jerry had already bought a beaten-up Victorian mansion that had survived being a nursing home and a college hangout – "there were 700 beer cans nailed to the wall," Jerry recalls. They were restoring that old place. Buying another property was too daunting.

"The Boutin mansion was a much grander home in comparison, in way better shape, with amazing woodwork and stained glass. It sat on a magnificent site, with few of the signs of disrespect we were dealing with at the time. Try as we might to contain it, our envy was palpable. But we didn't buy it."

They kept returning to Bayfield, and the mansion remained on the market, the price dropping temptingly. "When we first looked at the property, it was 40K. In 1971, it was 30K. When we came in 1972, it had just sold for 22K, interest-free with no money down. That's when we finally realized what a crazy outrageous value it was and that we should have bought it. It was a castle for the price of a cottage. So we really kicked ourselves," Jerry laments. "The following year of 1973 we came back to see the one that got away. We actually went through it on a paid tour for $3.50 a person and heard an organ concert."

Still stinging from not buying the Boutin mansion, they spied a 1800s Victorian mansion on Bayfield's main street for sale. "That was the year the Fuller mansion, the building that would become the Old Rittenhouse Inn, was for sale. It was in incredible condition, so we bought it! No doubt one thing that tipped us into buying it was that we were up to our elbows and earlobes redoing the old house in Oregon. We walked into the Fuller house and saw that incredible wood in mint condition and thought, 'Beautiful, beautiful, beautiful!' We just sat down on the porch to talk and it dawned on us we had to do this."

Mary and Jerry were not about to lose another opportunity. They drove down to Mert Heuer's real estate office and slipped an envelope under his door with five $100 bills.

"No doubt God works in strange ways. We missed buying the Château by two weeks, but when I think about the work that it needed, I suspect God was looking out for us because the Fuller house was in beautiful shape, ready to go. It had a brand-new roof. There was work done on the lawns, and new bathrooms. There were linens and silverware in the cupboards, and even a bottle of Dom Perignon in the refrigerator! And there was great curb appeal, sitting right there on Rittenhouse Avenue. Everybody drove by it twice."

At first they were content to have this beautiful "seasonal" home to visit on their increasingly frequent trips to Bayfield. They began to fill it with antiques. In summer, Jerry ran the Bayfield Inn dining room and bar.

With obvious room to spare, Mary and Jerry were occasionally asked to take in overnight guests when other town lodgings filled up. In the mornings, the couple shared their own coffee, muffins and summer fruits with these guests. They enjoyed the conversation and the questions. They became interested in learning what brought travelers to Bayfield.

In turn, the houseguests were interested in hearing about plans for the house. Those first guests, who paid whatever they could afford, lingered over morning coffee and offered advice on everything from wiring the antique light fixtures to restoring the parquet flooring. They inspired a business that would become the Old Rittenhouse Inn.

In these guests, Mary and Jerry found like-minded souls who also enjoyed traveling to meet new people, try new foods and experience different cultures. This kind of guest preferred a fireplace and a good conversation to a television (something we still believe today, and why we don't have TVs at the Inn).

Mary and Jerry discussed becoming full-time innkeepers. When the oil crisis of the mid-1970s hit – skyrocketing heating fuel costs into the stratosphere – they had to choose between the house in Oregon or the old Queen Anne Victorian mansion in Bayfield. They still had jobs in Madison, of course, and Jerry had also taken on work there with juvenile delinquents in a group home.

Sunshine – and sunny smiles – greet guests at the Inn's breakfasts. The sunshine depends on the weather; the smiles are there, regardless of the atmospheric mood outside.

Jerry and Mary had heard of bed-and-breakfast inns, which were becoming popular on the East Coast, but they had yet to reach Wisconsin. They knew that across the country, Victorian mansions were becoming an endangered species – too large for modern single-family dwellings and too expensive to maintain. Yet they were architecturally irreplaceable. Mary and Jerry thought they could save at least one. They chose the one in Bayfield.

In early 1975, they left the security of city jobs, packed up their only child (me) and the family belongings to move north to their new venture – the "Old Rittenhouse Inn," named for its location on Bayfield's main street, Rittenhouse Avenue.

Running a business in a remote small town presents surprises and challenges. It was years before gasoline or groceries were available on Sundays. We had to plan ahead, borrow or make do. Survival depended on turning problems into opportunities, and that became our mantra.

At first we all lived in the Rittenhouse, but eventually moved out and used all of the space for guests, which lead to the purchase of Grey Oak in 1987 and what Mom and Dad call the Gingerbread House in 1992.

Over the years, Mary and Jerry added more properties. They bought a building near the Inn and started an antique store, Rittenhouse Memories, in 1978. They purchased another antique store, Carriage Antiques, in Hayward in 1979. In 1985, they started an addition on the

Inn and purchased the Boutin mansion (the one that got away), which came up for sale later that year. In 1994, they bought Rittenhouse Cottage for a total of three lodgings under the Old Rittenhouse Inn umbrella.

We've since closed and sold the antique stores. The Bayfield building, owned by Bill and Sally Heytens, now houses "Ethel's at 250" – a great pizza and pasta restaurant. They live above the restaurant and it's become the perfect little model for how people with a vision can transform a space and make it functional and viable again.

We've enjoyed many challenges and accomplishments in our family businesses. One, of course, was creating a respected restaurant inside Old Rittenhouse Inn. Perhaps I'm most proud that the Landmark Restaurant and our creative chefs – starting with my mom, Mary – value and celebrate the local food bounty. We serve a wide range, from newly gathered wild blueberries to fresh-from-the-Big-Lake whitefish to apples from local orchards or red raspberries still sun-warmed from the neighbor's garden.

The idea for the Landmark started small. When we first began serving food, Mary quickly discovered that her small kitchen couldn't handle all of her breakfast ideas. The kitchen – and the menu – were expanded, adding lunch and dinner. The restaurant brought new responsibilities. Jerry baked the breads and desserts during the day, leaving him free to greet and serve customers in the evening. Mary took charge of all the cooking, plus handled reservations, dealt with utilities and vendors and answered every telephone call. She also created signature dishes we serve to this day. The availability of fresh ingredients inspired a frenzy of creation, recipe testing and tasting.

Landmark Restaurant's course became clear: local foods creatively prepared to their best advantage. That goal remains constant today. It's a big focus of what you will see among the recipes on the following pages. Bon appetit and tasty reading!

# Breakfast

# Smoked Lake Trout Frittata

Serves 4
Prep Time: 10 minutes
Cook Time: 30 minutes

## Ingredients

12 eggs
1 teaspoon salt
1 teaspoon pepper
1 cup heavy cream
1 red pepper, julienned
1 cup smoked lake trout, flaked
3 green onions, sliced
1/2 cup aged white cheddar, grated

**Chef's tip:** Be sure to use a nonstick pan or a very well greased pan so frittata will come out with ease after baking.

## Instructions

Preheat oven to 350° F. Whisk eggs, cream, salt and pepper. Grease a large oven-safe sauté pan and add the egg mixture. Top with red peppers and smoked trout. Bake approximately 25 minutes. After cooking, sprinkle with grated cheese and garnish with green onion.

*Gregg Thompson*

*Christian Giannelli*

# A la Crème Scramble

Serves 4-6
Prep Time: 10 minutes
Cook Time: 20 minutes

# Ingredients

12 eggs
2 sprigs basil, julienned
2 sprigs thyme, stemmed
1 teaspoon salt
1 teaspoon pepper
1 cup Roasted Mushrooms (See the recipe on page 156)
1 cup sour cream, divided
1/2 cup aged white cheddar, grated

> **Chef's tip:** I like to use mushrooms that have already been roasted, this way I don't have to wait 30 minutes for my eggs.

# Instructions

Grease a large sauté pan and place it on the burner over medium-low heat. Crack eggs into a mixing bowl. Add basil, thyme, 1/4 cup sour cream, salt, pepper and mushrooms. Add mixture to hot sauté pan and cook at medium-low until eggs are scrambled. Top with cheese and dollops of the remaining sour cream. Serve piping hot.

# Banana Rum Pancakes

Serves 4-6
Prep Time: 10 minutes
Cook Time: 10 minutes

## Ingredients

1 cup flour
1 teaspoon salt
1 teaspoon baking soda
1 egg
1-1/8 cup buttermilk
2 Tablespoons melted butter
3 bananas, sliced
1 jar of Old Rittenhouse Inn's Butter Rum Sauce, use 1/4 cup per serving
   (our sauce available online or substitute butterscotch or caramel ice-cream topping)

## Instructions

Preheat and lightly grease a large skillet or electric griddle. Mix flour, salt, and baking soda in a bowl. Add the egg, buttermilk and melted butter. Stir together lightly, leaving it a bit lumpy. The batter should look thick, spongy and puffy. Pour batter onto skillet/griddle to make 6-inch pancakes, using about 1/4 cup per pancake. Arrange slices of bananas on top of each. Cook a few minutes per side. Drizzle warmed rum sauce over pancakes just prior to serving.

# Rittenhouse Quiche

Serves 6-8
Prep Time: 20 minutes
Cook Time: 45 minutes

## Ingredients

1 9-inch pie shell, unbaked
1 onion, julienned
2 Tablespoons canola oil
2 Tablespoons sugar
1/2 cup fresh spinach
1/2 cup parmesan cheese, grated
2 cups heavy cream
4 eggs
1 teaspoon salt
1 teaspoon pepper

> **Chef's tip:** Be sure to sweat all of the water out of onions and spinach. If not, your quiche will not set up properly.

## Instructions

Preheat oven to 350° F. Combine onion, oil, and sugar in a sauté pan and cook over medium-low heat for about 10 minutes to caramelize the onions. Add spinach and wilt with the onions. Place onions, spinach, and cheese into the pie shell. In a mixing bowl, whisk cream, eggs, salt and pepper. Pour egg mixture into the pie shell and bake for about 40 minutes until middle of quiche is set. Let quiche cool 20 minutes. Slice, place on the plate and garnish with Red Pepper Rouille (see recipe page 168) and perhaps slices of orange or asparagus as shown here.

# Sausage-Apple French Toast

Serves 8
Prep Time: 20 minutes
Cook Time: 60-70 minutes

## Ingredients

3/4 pound pork sausage
2 medium apples, cored, peeled and cut into slices
6 eggs
2-1/2 cups milk
1/3 cup maple syrup
1/2 teaspoon nutmeg
20 slices French bread (or try cinnamon raisin bread), 1 inch thick

## Instructions

Cook sausage over medium heat until it is no longer pink. Drain, remove from skillet and set aside. Add apples to skillet, cover and cook for 3-5 minutes, or until tender, stirring occasionally.

In a bowl, whisk the eggs, milk, maple syrup and nutmeg until combined.

Grease a 9x13-inch or 11x14-inch baking dish and arrange half of the bread slices to cover the bottom. Pour half of the egg mixture over the top of it. Add a layer of sausage and apples. Cover with the remaining bread slices. Pour the remaining egg mixture over the bread layer, cover with foil, and refrigerate for up to 8 hours.

Preheat oven to 350° F. Place baking dish with foil in the oven for 30 minutes, remove foil and bake 30-40 minutes longer. Serve with Apple Maple Syrup (see below) and whipped cream.

---

**Apple Maple Syrup**
2 cups maple syrup
6 cinnamon sticks
1 cup frozen apple juice concentrate

Combine all ingredients in a saucepan and simmer over medium heat for 15 minutes. Remove cinnamon sticks and serve warm syrup with your favorite pancakes or French toast.

# Sweet & Spicy Breakfast Bacon

Serves 4
Prep Time: 5 minutes
Cook Time: 10 minutes

## Ingredients

8 bacon strips
1 teaspoon chili powder
1/8 teaspoon curry powder
1/8 teaspoon cayenne pepper
1/8 teaspoon cinnamon
3 Tablespoons maple syrup

## Instructions

Combine dry seasonings and sprinkle over both sides of bacon. Place bacon on an ungreased baking sheet. Drizzle with the maple syrup. Turn bacon and drizzle with remaining syrup. Bake at 400° F for 6-10 minutes until browned. Remove and blot with paper towel to remove extra grease from bacon before serving.

## Fond of Fiddleheads

In spring, we serve fiddlehead ferns for breakfast and dinner. When they're fresh, we buy all we can and then blanch and freeze for later what we can't use immediately.

Fiddlehead ferns are a great green vegetable that can substitute for beans, asparagus, or other greens as a side dish. They are great with garlic butter – but then, what isn't?

They do have an iron or mineral flavor on their own (especially noticeable when raw), which can be enhanced or mitigated by various cooking methods, depending on your desired effect.

My favorite use for fiddlehead ferns is on pizza (no joke!). They even look good on a pizza crust, just like little bright green heads on the necks of violins. And there is something about the interaction of the ferns with the sauce and cheese that makes everything extremely tasty when served this way. ∾

# Poached Eggs & Fiddlehead Ferns
## with Lake Superior Golden Caviar

Some years ago nearly all of the caviar made from Lake Superior whitefish and herring was shipped to northern Europe, where it is spread on toast with butter for breakfast. Our chef expanded on this theme by incorporating elements of a more American-style breakfast. This recipe is loaded with local flavors that are clearly reminiscent of the Northwoods. Sorghum is a Wisconsin country product similar in flavor to molasses. This caviar (American Golden) is plentifully produced in Bayfield. Fiddleheads are in such great supply here in the spring that we offer them in many dishes during their growing season.

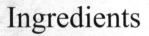

Serves 4
Prep Time: 15 minutes
Cook Time: 20 minutes

## Ingredients

8 slices Sorghum Rye Bread, cut in 3-inch rounds (see recipe on page 45)
8 eggs
splash of lemon juice or white wine vinegar
1/2 cup crème fraîche
2 teaspoons chopped Fines Herbes (buy premade or use equal parts fresh parsley, chives, tarragon and chervil)
1/2 cup fiddlehead ferns, with 2-3 inches of stem attached
2 Tablespoons butter, cubed
salt and pepper to taste
1/4 cup Lake Superior whitefish caviar (or American Golden caviar)

## Instructions

Mix Fines Herbes with crème fraîche and a pinch of salt. Reserve a couple snipped chives for garnish. Toast bread while poaching eggs for about 3 minutes in barely simmering salted water with a splash of white wine vinegar or lemon juice.

Sauté fiddleheads in butter over medium heat with salt and pepper to taste. Arrange toast on plate. Place an egg on each slice and top with a spoonful of caviar. Garnish with fiddleheads and drizzle crème fraîche on the plate.

# Cinnamon French Toast
## with Apricot Riesling Sauce

In 2005 the Old Rittenhouse Inn's new executive chef, David Miller, was surprised to learn that Bayfield grows delicious apricots. "Of course Bayfield is known for its apples and berries, but apricots?" he said, "On the shores of Lake Superior?"

Actually, it's the very Lake that makes it possible. The "lake effect" of Lake Superior creates an almost ideal growing climate for a short, but very productive, season for a wide variety of tree fruits, including apples, pears, and yes, apricots.

The Old Rittenhouse Inn has always made an effort to showcase regional cuisine. We have challenged our chefs to incorporate the delicious local ingredients into their recipes. This recipe begins with a long-standing favorite at the Rittenhouse breakfast table:

mouth-watering cinnamon-swirl French toast. We often serve this French toast with an array of fresh seasonal fruit sauces, including this delightful Apricot Riesling Sauce created by Chef Mark Wolslegel.

Serves 4
Prep Time: 15 minutes
Cook Time: 20 minutes

# Ingredients

1 cup milk
4 eggs
1/4 cup sugar
1/2 teaspoon vanilla extract
8 slices fresh cinnamon bread, 1 inch thick
1 small pat of butter

# Instructions

Whisk milk, eggs, sugar and vanilla extract until very smooth. Soak bread in mixture and drain off excess. Melt butter in skillet over medium heat. Cook French toast until golden brown and top with Apricot Riesling Sauce (recipe below).

_____

**Apricot Riesling Sauce**
1 cup Riesling wine
1/3 cup sugar
2-inch cinnamon stick
1/2 lemon, juiced
6 apricots, pitted, freshly sliced

Bring wine, sugar, cinnamon, and lemon juice to a boil. Remove cinnamon stick and add apricots. Immediately take off heat and let stand 5 minutes. Lightly stir, and serve over French toast.

# General Fuller

Since this ample beef-based dish makes you "generally fuller," we just had to make a play on words with the name of the Civil War general who built the Rittenhouse: Allen C. Fuller.

Serves 4
Prep Time: 10 minutes
Cook Time: 20 minutes

## Ingredients

3-5 Yukon Gold potatoes, 3/8-inch diced, peeled and parboiled
1 Tablespoon olive oil
pinches of salt and pepper
1 Tablespoon canola oil
1 red pepper, julienned
1 small red onion, julienned
1 pound beef tips
1/2 cup dry white wine
1 Tablespoon Dijon mustard
1/4 cup aged white cheddar, grated
8 fried eggs (optional) we recommend over easy, sunny side up or basted

> **Chef's tip:** Preheat the pan so it is nice and hot to get a good sear on your beef.

## Instructions

Place potatoes, olive oil, salt and pepper in large sauté pan and cook until browned. Preheat a second sauté pan with canola oil. Sauté peppers and onions for 3-4 minutes. Add beef and salt and pepper to taste. Cook another 3-4 minutes. Add wine and reduce by 75 percent. Stir in mustard. Place beef/veggie mixture over potatoes and top with cheese and optional fried eggs.

Residence of Frank Boutain,
Bayfield, Wis.

Dear Old Friend of
days gone by,
Have You forgotten
quite,
The jolly times we
used to have;
If not—Why don't you
Write?

# Quite the Attraction

What we call Le Château today has drawn attention since it was first built in 1908 by Frank Boutin.

These old postcards, once sold in Bayfield shops, show how the residence was worth writing home about.

While we've got the "General Fuller" breakfast named for the man who built the residence that became Old Rittenhouse Inn, we have yet to name a menu item for Mr. Boutin.

Perhaps an egg dish with house-smoked "Frank" might be appropriate. Any other ideas would be welcomed!

# *My Historic Siblings*

## Love on the Rebound

I've long realized that although I'm technically an only child, my folks consider their historic houses their "babies," too. That makes me a sibling, I guess, to the Rittenhouse and Boutin mansions. As you read earlier, Jerry and Mary almost didn't adopt those Victorian houses. The serendipity of finding the one after losing the other points to the path that was meant for our family.

Often my parents are asked what attracts them to Victorian-era homes. They've bought and restored several with large investments of time and money. Part of the charm, Jerry says, is what they represent. The Victorian period – the reign of Queen Victoria in England from 1837 to 1901 – marked the Industrial Revolution and the rise of a middle class. New manufacturing methods turned out mass quantities of goods, like affordable furnishings, and the increased incomes allowed families to invest in homes. The results – structures and products – are, Jerry says, "sometimes gaudy, but sometimes beautiful, rich complex-looking, delightful things."

Victorian homes feature astonishing space with ceilings reaching 8 or 11 feet, even in small rooms. With artisan labor still cheap, home builders could commission curves and corners, turrets and towers that could never be afforded by most today. There's a feeling of elegance in these old houses.

Today, under the umbrella of the Old Rittenhouse Inn operation, we own three of the historically significant structures in a 50-block area of Bayfield designated as a Historic District on the National Register of Historic Places in 1981. Old Rittenhouse Inn, Le Château and Rittenhouse Cottage each have their own story. We undertake our role as stewards of this living history with joy, gratitude … and a few terrifying mortgages.

## The Inn

The mansion today known as Old Rittenhouse Inn was originally started in 1890 and completed in 1892 as a summer home for Civil War Adjutant General Allen C. Fuller and his wife, Mary. Besides his military service, General Fuller was a judge and a member of the house and senate in Illinois.

The Fullers spent several summers in Bayfield, partly to relieve the general's hay fever or asthma. The couple bought property perched on a knoll overlooking Rittenhouse

From the front, Old Rittenhouse Inn looks much the same as in this early photo.

Avenue. The town's main street was named for Charles Rittenhouse of Philadelphia, one of the original businessmen to invest in building Bayfield. After Allen Fuller's death, his widow moved to Bayfield year-round and had central heat installed in the house. She stayed until her death around 1920.

The next owner, Dr. Mertens, bought the house for his home and clinic. He used two of the downstairs rooms for his practice through the mid-1940s. After him, Nettie Wilson and her sister, Agnes Meyers, owned the house. They rented rooms to teachers for about 20 years, then sold the house around 1960 to Allan Harbort from Milwaukee, who rented rooms in the summer and returned to Milwaukee for winters.

The home was again sold around 1969 to a LaCrosse businessman, Richard Morris, as a summer home. He spent a good deal of money repairing the roof, porches and fireplaces. Though he owned homes in several states, he told my parents that the Fuller house was the only home he ever really loved.

When my parents bought the building in 1973, it had not suffered the benign neglect of other historic buildings in the city. It was in excellent condition. They immediately started adding their favorite antiques and searching for key pieces to finish off the look of this incredible Queen Anne Victorian. "It's not like we had a grand business plan," Jerry recalls, "but it was a better choice for beginning what we eventually did have – a country inn. It had curb appeal on Rittenhouse Avenue, and it really worked out well roomwise with beginning a B&B. There was potential for a restaurant with space for parking. The only problem was

it was a residential property. At first that didn't bother us. It was only when we decided to put in a commercial kitchen and got our building permit that it became an issue.'"

The city realized the error, and Jerry and Mary got called before the Bayfield City Council to answer tough questions about starting a business in a residential neighborhood. Their ace in the hole, so to speak, was that they already had a building permit, signed by the responsible city official. It clearly stated that they were building a commercial kitchen. "How did we get this permit," Mary asked the council, "if it was inappropriate?"

The council reluctantly saw her point and rezoned our property, something rarely done in those days. We were spot zoned as commercial with no objections from the neighbors. Thus we officially began the Old Rittenhouse Inn in 1975, and in July 1976, we opened what is now the Landmark Restaurant, with dining in the first-floor parlor and sitting rooms.

Within a decade, the popularity of the business meant the need for more space. "It was 1985, and business was doing well," Jerry recalls. "We were featured on the cover of *Gourmet Magazine*, and the phones didn't stop ringing. When our rooms were completely booked and the phones kept ringing, we realized we had to expand."

This was an exciting time for the Inn. Business was good, things were looking up, and my parents took out a substantial loan to expand the Rittenhouse. They contacted several architects, but the ideas were either to tack a box onto the back of the building or create something out of character. "That wasn't what we had in mind," says Jerry. "So finally I drew some ideas and had them turned into blueprints by an architect."

Halfway through completion, Jerry decided something still wasn't quite right. "It was sort of a rectangle on the back, and as it was going up, we realized how ugly it was. That was where the idea for the octagon and the tower came."

Jerry drew his new ideas on graph paper, creating an octagon-shaped tower to give the exterior a more planned, finished look while adding another luxury suite on the third floor. The architect revised the plans. The quarter-million-dollar job became a half-million-dollar job … but the bank (thankfully) was very good about that. The original addition would have added four guest rooms, but as these things often go, the project quickly grew into something bigger. We ended up more than doubling our rentable rooms and expanded the kitchen and storage areas.

On a personal note, the construction site became my playground during the workers' time off. I explored in the giant foundation hole, climbed the bare bones of the addition and even sat on the very top of the Inn, looking out over Bayfield and the Apostle Islands. Let me tell you, it's one beautiful view.

Room II

Room III

There were four original bedrooms in the house. The Inn's Room I and Room II together were originally the home's master bedroom.

Room I

Room IV

The bed with the high headboard in Room IV was handcrafted by Carl Savitsky, who was working as a waiter in our restaurant at the time he made it. It remains one of our favorite pieces in the Inn. Rooms V and VI were created as part of the addition to the Inn.

Room VI

Room V

Room VIII

Room VII

Room IX

Suite XII – the Moroccan Suite – was the final bedroom finished after the addition. My parents had lived in this space for years. The unfinished, plain white walls drove Dad crazy at the time; he said the angular odd ceiling lines of the roof made it "like living in a tent." The remodeled space now echoes a sultan's tent, filled with treasures, just as traveling Victorian families gathered as souvenirs.

Suite XI

Moroccan Suite

# Suite Memories

There is an old picture that I love, not because of its great composition, but because it captures a memory. The photo, taken in what was then my third-floor bedroom, shows the Rittenhouse Singers in full song. In those days, the group rehearsed there and used it as a "green room," where they were outfitted with costumes (and warmed up) before performing a Wassail Dinner Concert.

I enjoyed having the choir in "my" room. Many in the photo are friends to this day, and a few are still in Jerry's choir. The group singing is part of the photo's charm, but the setting behind them really makes me nostalgic. My bedroom was plastered with rock 'n' roll posters and pages cut from music magazines. I had aspirations of being in a rock band and these rock groups were my other musical heroes. The photo blends my teen aspirations with my parents' promotion of music and the arts.

I loved that room. As a boy, it was the ballroom of my castle on the hill. But all kids leave their rooms (and homes) at some point. It's a rite of passage. They go off to college, or wherever, and their parents turn their bedroom into a guest room. In my case, my wonderful bedroom was converted into the opulent Rittenhouse Suite X, an Inn favorite.

My folks loved to renovate buildings even before we moved to Bayfield and over the years we lived in a series of homes around town: the Rittenhouse, the Silvernail Guest House across the street from the Inn, and the Goldman house, a cute gingerbread-trimmed house beside the Inn's Rittenhouse Cottage. Our family engaged in a more or less choreographed dance between rooms – shuffling into and out of them as we added guest space. The process happened over and over until all the rooms were finished – and then we'd buy another house.

As an adult, I see how commendable a goal it was for my parents, and now for Wendy and me, to restore the buildings and make them viable businesses to preserve them for the future. But I must admit a bit of nostalgia for my teen haven each time I see that photo of the Rittenhouse Singers … or whenever I show a guest into Suite X.

# Rittenhouse Cottage

A two-story, arts-and-crafts style house just one block from Old Rittenhouse Inn has become a secluded, one-of-a-kind Bayfield lodging and something of a family heirloom.

The Rittenhouse Cottage, as we call it, was built in 1911 and owned by the John Boehme family. John's daughter, Merle, was a housekeeper at the Inn for more than 20 years. When her father passed away, she asked us to buy the house to "keep it in the family," so to speak. It is a gorgeous little home, and we gladly agreed. For many years after, Merle continued to clean and care for her dad's old house.

One of our favorite features of the property is the cute little cow barn behind the house. In Bayfield during the 1800s, it was legal for each family to keep a cow or two to provide milk for the household. There were cow barns all over town, and this one, quite large and pretty, is one of the nicest still standing. The joke around town is that it's the only cow barn with an indoor toilet, which is true! John used the barn as his workspace and he had it plumbed.

I didn't know John well, but I remember him as one of those iconic senior citizens that everyone appreciates. He was a good carver and made whistles out of willow branches, which he gave to us kids in the summer at the Coast Guard Park by the lake.

Renovations on the house were fairly extensive and, as with all buildings, improvements are ongoing. In 2013, we added central heat & air conditioning. We also replaced the front porch, and then painted the exterior. It's just a cozy treasure that we enjoy sharing with travelers just as John shared his carving skills with us children.

Rittenhouse Cottage's lofted bedroom has a king bed and private bath with whirlpool tub and shower. An optional second king room, perfect for families or traveling couples, has a private bath with a tub/shower. Guests at the Cottage also enjoy the welcoming living room with a fireplace, wet bar and mini-refrigerator. The house has central air and is large enough to accommodate roll-away cots for additional guests. It is secluded and romantic, the perfect solution for a private wedding night or honeymoon.

# Le Château

The Boutin mansion was built by a Canadian immigrant to the United States. Frank Boutin Sr. moved first to Michigan and ultimately settled in Bayfield with his family of 14. He ran the local general store where the Madeline Island Ferry Terminal building is today. Eventually he got into the lumbering business and built a sawmill.

The business really took off, though, under the leadership of his eldest son, Frank Boutin Jr. The Boutins captured the essence of what it takes to make a million dollars: Cut out all the middle people because *you are* the middle people. They ran the mill and owned a fleet of boats that transported their lumber (and that of the other local mills) to market.

Flush with timber profits and wanting to impress his New York bride, Frank Jr. purchased property to build a mansion on the Bayfield hill, overlooking the lumber mill and general store. The house he built in 1908 exemplified the Queen Anne Victorian style of architecture with sweeping porches, a corner turret, dormer windows and a complex gabled roof. It also features stained-glass windows, quarter-sawn oak paneling and a wraparound front porch with a commanding view of Lake Superior.

Le Château was the first private home in Bayfield to have electricity, brought by Boutin on his own line because at the time the only electric line running up Rittenhouse Avenue was for main street businesses. The home's foyer was lit by Edison bulbs and a globe chandelier. (Many of the vintage bulbs still function today!)

Boutin endowed his mansion with all the latest gadgets. We love the brass-and-

Early Bayfield postcards featured the Boutin mansion.

Ballroom

Master Suite

North Room

Northeast Room

Le Château rooms are named for direction or their original use by the Boutin family.

copper fuse box that once ran the Château's electrical systems. We also love the electric call system, based in the kitchen, that placed little buttons throughout the house that allowed the owners to call the staff for help.

Perhaps because he grew up with 13 siblings, Boutin installed bathrooms on every floor – a highly unusual luxury in those days. Unfortunately, the beautiful porcelain tile in those original bathrooms was embedded in eight inches of solid concrete, along with the water pipes. Years of freeze-thaw cycles caused pipes to break inside the concrete and ultimately the tiles were lost. This was one of many priority projects after our family purchased the property in 1986. (More on this in a minute.)

The lumber supply dwindled in this area much faster than anticipated, harvested out in 20 years instead of 50. Boutin was left saying, "Here I am, sitting in Bayfield when it's all moving West!" So he sold the house and built another in St. Paul, overlooking the Capitol. He tried to get into banking, but eventually moved to Portland, Oregon, where he's listed as being in charge of up to 10 different lumber companies.

The second owners of the house were from Chicago and had connections to rum runners during Prohibition. There are stories of locals delivering groceries – fish, apples, cider, coal, etc. – to the house and being met at the door by a guard with a Tommy gun.

When Prohibition was repealed in 1933, the bootleggers didn't need the house anymore, so it was given to the Catholic Church for $1. At the time, the numbers at the Catholic school and orphanage were dwindling, so they tore down the convent and orphanage, left the school and moved the nuns into the Boutin mansion, which became their convent for the next 35 years.

Two of the Boutin sisters, Ronnie in front & Mata in back, at their home.

Not knowing the mansion belonged to the church, Mary and Jerry were surprised to be greeted by a nun.

"She was very cordial and showed us around the first floor. We walked into this grand old house and said, 'Wait a second … the nuns are living in this place?'" laughs Jerry. "There were kneelers in several of the rooms where they would pray. I don't remember much about that first visit because it was so dark in there. It was like curtains upon curtains, and the windows gave so little light. I just remember this incredibly nice wood, but it was so dark."

The building needed repair, and for the church, it wasn't worth keeping up. The nuns had recently moved into the rectory with the students and priests.

"I always thought that was odd," says Jerry of the residential mix. "I later asked one of the priests about living with the nuns, and he said, 'There's no problem as long as you don't get into the habit.'" (I can't vouch for the veracity of this last line, but it's how Jerry always tells the story.)

South Room

The outdoor pergola and fountain gardens have become a favorite site for wedding ceremonies. The outside lawn, as well as many of the rooms, offer great views of Lake Superior.

Turret Suite

Tower Room

It was more than a decade after buying the Rittenhouse that we purchased the Boutin mansion, along with all of its massive repair needs.

As I mentioned earlier, one priority project was fixing damage caused by frozen pipes. I was 15 years old and got the job of breaking up tile and concrete with a sledgehammer, tossing it out a window into a chute that directed the rubble down to a pickup truck. Those were long, hard days, and it was an awful job that required attention so as not to damage the beams. It was so sad to destroy all those beautiful porcelain tiles, though I kept a few as souvenirs.

We did make one good save. A previous owner had installed a pipe organ on the third floor. During restoration, we carefully took the organ apart and donated it to Messiah Lutheran Church in Washburn, where it was restored and remains part of the services to this day. That organ may have echoes in Le Château, too. One housekeeper reported hearing organ music emanating from that room on several occasions … long after the organ had been removed.

The Boutin house was a great project, but we desperately needed more cash. Beside the interior repairs, the roof was in shambles and it needed cleaning, rewiring, replumbing, etc. to get the rooms ready for guests. So we brought in a silent partner for cash, willing to get payback in the form of a tax break because our project was done with National Register Historic Trust tax credits. So our partner was happy, and we were happy because we could save the building.

We were so fortunate to have great partners, including the bank. You hear all these horror stories about working with partners, but for us they were wonderful relationships.

Eventually we bought a third property, the Rittenhouse Cottage. The quaint space can house up to five guests or gives perfect privacy for a wedding couple or the wedding party. Cottage guests love the lofted bedroom (with king bed) and the whirlpool tub.

Running one business on three sites can be a challenge. We want all of our guests, no matter which building, to feel part of the "Old Rittenhouse Inn Experience."

The way to do that, we've found, is at breakfast or brunch. Every guest begins with a day-opener at our Landmark Restaurant in the Inn – so our "Rittenhouse" family, as with so many families, comes together at the table.

# Guest Journal

Date of Stay _____

Occasion _____

Room _____

Notes _____

_____

_____

_____

_____

_____

_____

_____

_____

_____

_____

_____

_____

_____

_____

_____

_____

# Breads

# Wild Leek & Dill Bread

Yields 2 loaves or 2 dozen rolls
Prep Time: 1-2 hours
Cook Time: 45 minutes

## Ingredients

1 cup wild leeks, minced (or substitute green onions or chives)
1/4 cup fresh dill, minced
1/4 cup unsalted butter, melted
2 eggs, slightly beaten
1 Tablespoon active dry yeast
2 Tablespoons warm water (110-115° F)
1 Tablespoon fresh garlic, minced
1-1/2 teaspoons salt
3 Tablespoons sugar
2 cups lukewarm milk
3-4 cups all-purpose flour

> **Chef's tip:** The Wild Leek & Dill Bread recipe makes an awesome dough that makes great rolls (shown here), dinner muffins, round loaves or regular loaves. Make 1-inch dough balls for rolls. At Landmark, we usually turn the dill dough into easy-to-serve dinner muffins. As a round loaf, though, this bread will hold up well if scooped out for dips or thick soups.

## Instructions

Preheat oven to 350° F. In mixer bowl, combine warm water and yeast and let sit for 5 minutes. Add leeks, dill, butter, eggs, garlic, salt, sugar and milk. Slowly add flour with dough hook on low speed. Add enough flour until firm dough is formed. Continue on low to knead dough for 5 minutes. Cover and let double in size in warm place (about 40 minutes). Punch down and transfer dough into greased 9x5x3-inch bread pans and let double in size again until the dough is about 1 inch above the pan (about another 40-60 minutes). Bake 35-45 minutes.

# Cheddar & Bacon Buttermilk Biscuits

Yields 12 biscuits
Prep Time: 30 minutes
Cook Time: 30 minutes

## Ingredients

6 slices thick-cut bacon
3-3/4 cups all-purpose flour
1-1/2 Tablespoons baking powder
1-1/4 teaspoons salt
1/2 cup unsalted butter, chilled, cut into 1/2-inch cubes (plus more melted butter
  for brushing)
1-1/2 cups sharp cheddar, grated
1-3/4 cups buttermilk, chilled

## Instructions

Preheat oven to 425° F. Line large, heavy baking sheet with parchment paper. Cook bacon in large skillet over medium heat until crisp and brown. Transfer bacon to paper towel to drain and then chop coarsely. Combine flour, baking powder, baking soda and salt in food processor. Blend for 5 seconds. Add butter cubes. Blend until coarse meal forms (about 30 seconds). Transfer flour mixture into large bowl. Add cheese and bacon. Gradually add buttermilk, mixing until combined. Using lightly floured hands, drop generous 1/2-cup batter portions onto prepared baking sheet. Space portions 2 inches apart. Bake 18-20 minutes or until inserted toothpick comes out clean. Brush with melted butter and cool for 10 minutes.

# Apple Cinnamon
## Cream Cheese Muffins

Yields 8-10 muffins
Prep Time: 20 minutes
Cook Time: 15-17 minutes

## Ingredients

1-1/2 cups all-purpose flour
1/2 cup sugar
2 teaspoons baking powder
pinch of salt
1/2 cup vanilla yogurt
1/4 cup canola oil
1 egg
1 Tablespoon cinnamon
1 apple, peeled, cored and diced
4 ounces cream cheese
1 teaspoon vanilla
1/4 cup powdered sugar
1/4 cup coarse sugar (optional, also called pearl or decorating sugar)

## Instructions

Preheat oven to 350° F. Combine flour, sugar, baking powder and salt in mixing bowl. In smaller bowl, mix yogurt, oil and egg, then combine with flour mixture. Add apples and cinnamon. In a third bowl, beat cream cheese, vanilla and powdered sugar until blended. Grease muffin pan (or use paper muffin cups) and fill cups halfway with batter. Add 1 spoonful of cream cheese mixture to each muffin and cover each with remaining batter. Sprinkle with coarse sugar (optional). Bake 15-17 minutes.

# Roasted Red Pepper & Parmesan Rolls

Yields 12-14 rolls
Prep Time: 2 hours 30 minutes
Cook Time: 18-22 minutes

## Ingredients

1 cup red peppers, sliced and roasted
1 Tablespoon active dry yeast
2 Tablespoons warm water (110-115° F)
1 cup grated parmesan cheese, divided
1/4 cup warm milk (110-115° F)
2 Tablespoons butter, melted
1 teaspoon salt
2-3 cups all-purpose flour, divided
1 teaspoon pepper

## Instructions

Preheat oven to 350° F. Place red peppers in blender and purée. In mixer, dissolve yeast in
warm water. Add peppers, 1/2 cup of parmesan, milk, butter, salt and 3/4 cup flour. Beat with
dough hook until smooth. Add enough of the remaining flour to form a firm dough. Continue
kneading the dough on low for about 5 minutes. Cover and let rise in a warm place until
doubled in size (about 1 hour). Punch down, grease muffin pans and fill with 1-inch thick
dough balls. Add remaining cheese to tops of dough. Let rise one more time until doubled
(about 30 minutes). Bake for 18-22 minutes.

# Orange-Glazed Blueberry Scones

Yields 8-10 scones
Prep Time: 10 minutes
Cook Time: 50 minutes

## Ingredients

2 cups all-purpose flour (plus 1 Tablespoon more for rolling berries)
1 Tablespoon baking powder
1 teaspoon salt
1/3 cup sugar
1/4 cup unsalted butter, cubed
3/4 cup buttermilk or heavy cream
1 egg
1 pint fresh blueberries

## Instructions

Preheat oven to 400° F. In large bowl, sift together flour, baking powder, salt and sugar. Cut in butter using two forks or pastry blender. In another bowl, mix buttermilk and egg together. Add to flour mixture. Roll blueberries in flour to coat and fold into batter. (The flour keeps them from dropping to the bottom of the batter.)

Drop tablespoon-sized dollops of batter onto a ungreased cookie sheet. Bake 15-20 minutes. Cool before topping with glaze.

---

**Orange Glaze**
2 Tablespoons unsalted butter, melted
2 cups powdered sugar
2 oranges, zested and juiced

Combine all ingredients into a bowl. Top cooled scones with orange glaze. Let glaze harden for 15 minutes. (It's easiest to make the glaze after the scones have cooled.)

# Irish Soda Bread

Yields 1 loaf
Prep Time: 30 minutes
Cook Time: 25 minutes

## Ingredients

3 cups bread flour
1/3 cup sugar
1 teaspoon baking soda
1 teaspoon baking powder
3/4 teaspoon salt
2-1/2 sticks of unsalted butter, cold
1-1/2 cups buttermilk

## Instructions

Preheat oven to 400° F. Mix dry ingredients in a bowl.

Using the large holes of a cheese grater, grate butter into the dry ingredients. Toss butter with flour mixture just until it crumbles. Add buttermilk and lightly mix until combined. Place dough on a greased pan and sprinkle lightly with flour so it does not stick to your hands. Shape dough into a 10-inch disk that is about 1 inch thick. With sharp knife, cut an "X" across the top. Bake for 20-25 minutes

# Sorghum Rye Bread

Yields 3 loaves
Prep Time: 2 hours 30 minutes
Cook Time: 30-40 minutes

## Ingredients

3/4 cup sorghum flour
2 cups hot water
1-1/4 ounces yeast, instant (5 packages)
3 Tablespoons rye flour
1-1/2 cups bread flour

3/4 cup rye flour
1-1/4 cups bread flour
1 Tablespoon salt
2 Tablespoons unsalted butter, softened

cornmeal to dust on dough-rising tray
vegetable oil for brushing

> **Chef's tip:** Creating a sponge starter adds a tangy flavor and makes the bread slightly less dense.

## Instructions

Mix first 5 ingredients to a batterlike consistency for a sponge starter. Cover it and let rest until it becomes spongy and doubles in size (about an hour). Mix in remaining ingredients, let rest another 10 minutes. Portion into three pieces and shape into oval loaves on sheet tray dusted with cornmeal. Cover and let rise until doubled (about another hour) then bake at 350° F for 30-40 minutes. Use a toothpick to test for doneness; it should come out clean. The bread will have a nicely browned crust, which should be brushed lightly with vegetable oil after removing from the oven.

# Growing Up B&B

## New Day, Another Adventure

Every day is an adventure when you grow up in an Inn. Just for starters, consider the many rooms to explore and places to hide.

When we first moved to Bayfield, our family lived on the whole third floor of the Inn. The perk: Every window looked out over Bayfield and Lake Superior. The challenge: We used a woodstove for heat, and if someone didn't get up at 2 a.m. to fill it with logs, we'd all be half frozen by morning.

My first bedroom was in the house's ballroom (now the Inn's Suite X), so I had about 1,000 square feet in which to stretch out. I played Nerf football, pretending I was Bob Griese and the undefeated '72 Dolphins. With my best friend Kris, I staged mock lightsaber battles and "flew" my X-wing and TIE fighters.

The entire room features tongue-and-groove hardwood walls and ceiling, plus built-in bookcases line the walls. By my childhood calculations, there were at least a zillion books up there, and I spent hours in my room reading, drawing and playing. I had a lot of time to myself back then, being an only child, except for Mom and Dad's newest baby – their B&B business.

A B&B tills fertile soil for an active imagination, and while I spent a fair amount of time alone, my routine life easily became fantastical in my mind. One night, for example, Mom had a filet mignon sent up for my dinner. You might think, "How lucky for a kid to have filet mignon for dinner" and you'd be right – another benefit of living over a great restaurant – but I imagined something better. The steak became a freshwater octopus, dragged by me onto a Lake Superior beach and charred over an open fire by my plucky mom. (The downside to such luxury was no McDonald's, and, in truth, there wasn't one within 70 miles of Bayfield then. Luckily Mom kept a supply of the local Hugo's frozen pizzas, so I didn't have to suffer with filet mignon/wild octopus every night.)

My fun-loving parents tended and encouraged my imagination. As a Halloween-time baby, I got the best birthday parties in a Victorian home ready-made for treasure hunts, hide-and-seek, pin the tail on the ghost and a host of fun Rittenhouse Inn-only type games.

My imagination, of course, did not stop at the threshold of the Inn. On Saturday mornings, Dad would wrap me up in my blanket and carry me over to Grandma June Stuessy's house, across the street, where I watched cartoons. I really got into Tarzan. I can only imagine what Grandma June, who raised her only daughter on a farm in Brodhead,

*Julie Phillips*

*Joan Fitzgerald*

*Joan Fitzgerald*

Growing up in a house filled with guests made me comfortable being "on stage" as a Wassail Concert singer (bottom left), a horn-playing musician (top right), or striking a pose on our porch (center). That's me (top left) age 11, sometime just before my wild Phillips beard sprouted!

Wisconsin, must have thought of me stripping down to my tighty whiteys and jumping around the furniture, pounding my little chest and howling like a great ape.

Living where my parents worked, I learned early the value of labor. My first job at the Inn was stemming strawberries. Bayfield's location on a peninsula surrounded by Lake Superior gives it a unique microclimate favorable for farms to produce amazing berries and fruit all summer. To this day, strawberry season remains one of my favorite times of year and it's my son Max's favorite, too. He loves to eat those strawberries just as much as I did when Grandma Junebug and I would sit together, stemming crate after crate of berries (quite a few went straight into my mouth). Mom paid me 50 cents per flat, and I did about 10 flats at a time.

They loved me down at the five-and-dime because I bought so many football cards. One time, though, the clerk called Mom when I brought in $20, wondering where a kid my age might get that kind of cash. (A check-up-on-you phone call from a store clerk is a sure sign of small-town living.)

"He earned that money," Mom assured the clerk, whom I think felt badly for doubting me because she gave me free candy to go with my purchase that day.

In my early teen years, Old Rittenhouse Inn undertook an addition that doubled its size. Once the giant bulldozer scooped a massive space for the foundation, creating a big mudhole, I had my new "playground" as soon as the workers left for the day. When they framed in the first-floor bedrooms (now rooms 8 and 9), the kitchen addition and eventually the second-floor level (rooms 5, 6 and 7), the stage was set for my passion of the moment – ninjas.

Thin wooden slats used to mark construction zones became ninja swords for my friend Kris and me. In our imaginations, we filled in the invisible walls outlined by the framed areas and pretended we could walk through the walls or slice through them with our ninja swords.

Eventually the workers put in the third floor and the tower, giving us access to the roof. We'd climb to the tippy top of the Inn to look out over Bayfield and Lake Superior to the Apostle Islands and all the way to Michigan. Talk about king of the world! (Or in adult hindsight, talk about potentially dangerous!)

Today if we need to get up there for a roof repair or sweep a chimney, I'm happy to pay someone else to do it. I'm just not as big a fan of heights as I was in my carefree ninja days.

Grandma June Stuessy (top left) taught me how to read – and how to stem strawberries. After a very liberal education, I graduated (top right) in 1994 from the University of Wisconsin-Madison. Dad and me, circa 1991 (bottom).

*Matthew Kurtz*

# Under the Grand Piano

When my mom started teaching piano lessons during college, she got a big, beautiful 1850s Knabe grand piano from her mother. After college, Mom continued to give private music lessons. When we moved to Bayfield, the piano came with us. For many years, it sat where our front desk is today. The piano fit snugly there, and underneath was the perfect hiding spot for a young boy.

I loved spending time under that piano and kept most of my favorite toys there – Star Wars figures, Matchbox cars, Lincoln Logs, Legos and my prized Fisher Price castle. I'd play quietly there most evenings while guests dined only a few yards away. Most of the time, they didn't know I was there, but occasionally someone would spot me and say, "Look, there's a little boy playing."

*Phillips collection*

To this day, some returning guests comment about seeing me under that piano. These days the grand piano resides in Le Château's music room, still used for occasional concerts and wedding receptions.

Recently, I crawled under the grand piano to plug in a light, and I was amazed at how tight it was under there. I recalled a lot more room, but, then again, there was a lot less of me in those days.

# Zorro Strikes Again

Growing up in an Inn sometimes means personal exposure in ways not usually of concern in most households. In other words, there is no normal privacy.

For example, I vividly remember when I was about 5 watching TV in my third-floor bedroom when a promotional spot came on for an upcoming showing of "Zorro." Inspired to action, I tied a towel around my neck, grabbed a cardboard tube for a "sword" and a towel for a "whip". Excited to tell my parents all about it, I ran downstairs, past the dining guests and into the kitchen, whirling and slashing all the way.

"What is going on?" asked my mother, concern creasing her brow.

"Zorro's coming to TV soon, Mom!" I exclaimed.

"That's nice dear," she said, relieved, then added, "but next time, please put your pants on before you come downstairs."

# Many Thanks to the Villages
# (and the Villagers)

The old saying is true; it does take a village to raise a child. In my case, it took two villages, the "village" of Bayfield and the "village" of Hayward.

My parents' love has always surrounded me – they made it abundantly clear that I was the "best boy in the world," even on those days when maybe I wasn't. Their busy innkeeping schedules, though, made it harder to be available at times.

That's where the villages, filled with surrogate mothers, fathers, aunts and uncles, came to our aid. As a child, I spent more time in Hayward where my dad's shop, Carriage Antiques, was located. I attended school there from third grade through high school. Tony Aderman and Edwin Zalewski were classmates. They were also my neighbors, and we became fast friends. Whenever Dad had to be away at the Old Rittenhouse Inn, the Adermans and the Zalewskis became my surrogate families, helping to take care of me and to guide me.

I remember the Zalewskis as the quintessential clean-cut, hard-working American family – mom and dad, brother and sister. The boys had short '50s-style buzz cuts, high and tight. Mr. Z. smoked a pipe and taught history at Hayward High School. Mrs. Zalewski also taught. They had an International Harvester Scout that was often hauling a canoe or other gear on top or was loaded for a fishing or camping trip.

The Adermans, our other Hayward neighbors, would take me in for a whole week sometimes when Dad had to be in Bayfield. I always felt the Adermans would have been at home as frontier pioneers living off the land – or at least would be comfortable in the rugged landscape of Alaska, taming the wilderness.

Tony, who was my age, was a real outdoorsman and we went fishing whenever we could. He also took me trapping and hunting, experiences I would not have had without him.

In some ways, the Adermans started my awareness of interesting, good food. They kept an amazing garden, meticulously maintained and always free of weeds. Its high yield of produce was eaten fresh or canned for winter. Meals for the family of six also included a significant amount of fresh game.

The mother, Pat, was an amazing cook. I loved her "hobo dinner," cooked over an open fire in their outdoor kitchen.

The ingredients for a hobo dinner depended on the season. Pat would take a large five-gallon tin that cherries had come in and fill it with water, various seasonings, kielbasa sausage, potatoes, corn on the cob, carrots, onions, rutabagas or whatever was the freshest and best produce in season. She boiled it all over the fire. I still recall the inviting smell and the fantastic, fresh taste of that one-pot meal, scooped from the cherry tin and served at the table. It rapidly disappeared as we all tucked in.

Another memorable Aderman meal featured a giant snapping turtle. The jaws of the fierce old thing still snapped a broom handle three days after its demise! I've only tasted snapping turtle that one time, but Pat's snapping-turtle chop suey was memorably delicious – the best chop suey I've ever had in my life. The neatest part to the boyhood me was that the turtle meat still wiggled a bit in the bowl! The Aderman's daughter Beth definitely was not as thrilled by this as we boys were.

Me in my room, circa 1985 – just too cool for words!

Both sets of parents were strict with their children and expected obedience. Punishment came swiftly, but it was always fair; the discipline tempered with a lot of love – all the right ingredients for a family.

My Bayfield surrogates were family: my grandma and my aunty. Especially from the mid-1970s through the 1980s, when my parents scrambled to build their business, renovate their old houses and raise their only child.

A popular catch phrase of Mary's during this time was "After we turn the corner," as in, "After we turn the corner, we'll get a new car. For now, we'll have to make do."

Now that I'm doing the work of innkeeper and parent myself, I see it all more clearly. Wendy and I make every effort to carve out time for our children, but we still need the help of the village. Kyra and Max are bright and talented. One of them might even be interested in continuing the story of the Old Rittenhouse Inn someday. If not, we'll encourage them to pursue whatever fascinates them and to chase their dream wherever it takes them.

# Wendy & Me

Our family is now into the second generation of innkeepers – that would be my lovely, patient, innovative wife and me. Some days I think it's a good thing we "adopted" Wendy.

Wendy and I met in the summer of 1994 – my parents set us up, more or less.

After graduating from University of Wisconsin-Madison with a bachelor degree in English creative writing, I came home to work at Old Rittenhouse Inn for "one last summer" (that always makes me laugh) before moving out West.

Wendy was a sophomore studying music therapy at UW-Eau Claire. My parents hired her for a summer job at the Inn.

Wendy wasn't a newcomer; she'd worked in housekeeping while I was away at

*Randall Peterson*

Smiles all around for the family, from top: Me and my main squeeze at the county fair; Wendy kidding around at a photo shoot promoting the Old Rittenhouse Inn gift card; Kyra, me, Max and Wendy at home; Max and Kyra at a young age; and wee Kyra with Grandpa Jerry.

college. We hadn't crossed paths earlier, but when she was promoted to the wait staff, I was the maître d' in charge of training her.

Right away, we connected. With her big, beautiful smile, Wendy was (and is) the sweetest person I've ever met. I believe she took a shine to me, too. Unfortunately, we were dating other people then, so while we both felt that spark, we remained just friends that summer. Soon the high season was over, and Wendy was heading back to college. I had decided to postpone my trip West, to stick around a bit longer – you know, in case Mom and Dad needed help. Before she left, I told Wendy in passing that I was having my wisdom teeth extracted in September.

Away she went to Eau Claire. A few weeks went by, and on the day of my oral surgery, a card arrived in the mail. Wendy was thinking about me and wished me well on that not-fun day. I showed the card to Mom. "I approve," Mom said – not a phrase I heard much when it came to prospective girlfriends.

I next saw Wendy at our employee Christmas party. She was home for winter break and came to the staff party. We've been together ever since, and Mom still approves.

We've also started our third generation of innkeepers (if that's what they want). Kyra and Max constantly amuse and amaze us. Kyra takes after her great-grandmother and grandmother, already an avid reader at age 10. Max, 6, reminds me of my dad; happy-go-lucky and creative. They're not growing up quite so B&B as I did, since we don't live at the Inn. But Kyra and Max definitely know the Old Rittenhouse Inn as being part of the family. I hope one or both of them might consider taking it on as part of their future.

# Mom & Dad

Music teachers, performers, church musicians. Restorers of Victorian homes, defenders of historic public buildings, keepers of an inn, cooks and greeters. Mom and Dad. No need to list even a few of their accomplishments – I know my parents are amazing.

Our lives have always been hectic, but the time we spend together is rich and full. I can't imagine better, more creative parents than mine.

Guests loved my mother's gourmet cooking and the wonderful smells that emanated from our tiny kitchen where she made her magic. She worked from 4 a.m. to 11 p.m. most days, fueled by giant Eckels Pottery mugs filled to the brim with strong black coffee. (The local potter's work makes good coffee even more beautiful.)

My dad was the "front man" for Old Rittenhouse Inn, with his flamboyant ruffled shirts, prim vests and large velvety bow ties. So outfitted, he still cuts a dashing figure.

Jerry loves antiques and did much of the decorating at the Inn. What some don't know is that he is also a fantastic baker. In the afternoons, between meetings, he'd create delicious breads, cakes and pastries and favorite desserts like the Pot de Crème au Chocolat.

But once dinner service started, Dad was in the front of the house, welcoming guests and describing the night's dinner menu in mouthwatering detail. It was all part of the show, an over-the-top dinner experience that most of our guests had never seen the likes of before (or perhaps since).

I have a few stories – gleaned from among a lifetime of fond memories – that help to illustrate how extraordinary my parents truly are.

My mom is brilliant, and the perfect proof of this remains one of my best memories of college. I had a rough first semester (or rather I had a too-much-fun first semester) and my GPA suffered. The next semester, with no choice but to get better grades, I found myself in a difficult art history class with a demanding professor. To help, Mom gave me enough money for two copies of the books in that class – one for me and one for her. She knew me that well.

Hilary Cronon
Me, Wendy, Dad and Mom posing on the porch.

Weeks later, hopelessly stuck on a term paper, I phoned Mom. She was at the Inn cooking dinner, but said she had time to talk. The kitchen sounds in the background made me homesick.

I told her where I was stuck. She was silent for a moment, as if computing, then said, "Go to page 62 of your book. On the lower left page, at the bottom, the last paragraph. I think you'll find it there."

I immediately flipped to the page, and there was my answer. Mom didn't have the book in hand – more likely she held a spatula, a large spoon, a hot pan or a raw steak – but she could see the book in her head. She has that kind of an amazing memory.

To this day, Mom reads voraciously, keeping about six books going at once. She stashes them in different places around the house, and wherever she finds herself with a few free moments, she picks up a book and reads a chapter or two. Truly amazing.

Not to brag too much, but my dad, too, over and over shows how incredibly strong and resilient he is and how he lives on the bright side of life, even at the worst times.

When my grandfather died, Dad sang Schubert's "Ave Maria" at the funeral. It's emotional and extremely challenging to sing, but my dad nailed it. To this day, I've never heard the piece performed so well. How could Dad sing that song at his own father's funeral? I asked him. Dad admitted it was the hardest thing he ever did. He leaned on my mother, who accompanied him on the organ that day. She had encouraged him to sing at the service.

Family photo album: Left (Dad's side): Bud and Margaret Phillips' family (clockwise from top left) John, Joe, Janis, Joan, Jerry, Jim, Jill, Margaret, Jeff, Julie, Bud and Jean; Grandpa Bud Phillips at his first communion; Grandpa Bud and Grandma Margaret Phillips' wedding pose by a vintage car.

Right (Mom's side): Grandma June Stuessy as on the farm; Grandma June reading; Grandpa Herbert and Grandma June Stuessy.

"Mary had played at her own mother's funeral. I'd watched her go through the same thing and she handled it so well," Dad explained. "I realized it was important to do it, not just for my father, but for all the people who were left. It's essential to celebrate life, even during the saddest times."

"Genial Jerry" charms everyone with his infectious positive attitude. I've seen it hundreds of times when new guests come down for dinner. First-timers can be tentative, perhaps mildly intimidated by the Victorian atmosphere, the antiques, the vintage wallpapers.

Then Jerry welcomes them, asks where they're from, describes the night's menu and shares some house history. The guests relax. Often, after a great dinner and a nice bottle of wine, when Jerry returns to tell them about desserts, he can't get away from that table. They've fallen in love with their charismatic host who makes them feel like the only guests in the restaurant.

Jerry loves them in return and often makes lifelong friends. Joseph and Susan Nordstrom are great examples of this. The Nordstroms are repeat guests, coming every year (even though with five daughters it's not easy to get away).

One summer, Joe asked Mom, Dad and I to sit for a few photographs. He was thinking of quitting his "day job" to become a portrait artist and wanted us to be his first official subjects. I felt humbled by such an honor, but, honestly, after awhile I forgot all about the whole thing.

Three years later, Joe showed up with a large gift wrapped in brown paper. We were stunned; Joe painted a true-to-life likeness of our family on canvas. Because the portrait took "waaaaay too long" to finish, Joe said he decided to keep his "day job," making the gift all the more special.

The Nordstroms continue to visit every year and always stay at Le Château, where Joe can see his artwork, the featured portrait hanging in the music room.

Relationships like those we have with the Nordstroms illustrate the generosity of our guests and how Mom and Dad's work as innkeepers has been as extraordinary as the rest of their lives. They've received many awards, one of the most meaningful is the Wisconsin Bed and Breakfast Association's 2013 Presidents Award for, as it says on the award: "Your generosity of spirit. For sharing your insights, knowledge and humor. For your dedication to WBBA. For being the best example of a couple in love with each other and their work."

# Appetizers

# Bruschetta (Grilled Toast)

Serves 4
Prep Time: 15 minutes
Cook Time: 10 minutes

## Ingredients

1/2 cup fresh tomato, chopped
1 teaspoon garlic, chopped (plus a sliced clove for rubbing)
1 Tablespoon red onion, minced
2 Tablespoons olive oil
3 Tablespoons fresh basil, chopped (6-10 leaves)
2 Tablespoons Kalamata olives, diced
splash of lemon juice or vinegar
pinches of salt and cracked black pepper
4 slices French bread or sourdough baguette
Shredded parmesan and mozzarella as topping (optional)

## Instructions

Combine above ingredients (except cheese and bread). Take slices of bread and rub with the sliced garlic clove. Grill dry (no butter or oil) until toasted. Cover toasted bread with mixture. Top with cheeses. Finish in warm oven to melt cheese.

# Seared Smoked Scallops

Serves 4
Prep Time: 20 minutes
Cook Time: 25 minutes

## Ingredients

8-12 jumbo scallops
2 Tablespoons paprika
1 Tablespoon chili powder
1 Tablespoon ground coriander
2 Tablespoons brown sugar
1 Tablespoon ground thyme
1 Tablespoon juniper berries
1/2 Tablespoon kosher salt
1 teaspoon pepper
1 Tablespoon olive oil
salt and pepper to season
1/2 pound soaked wood chips (applewood works best)

> **Chef's tip:** I prefer to use charcoal instead of an electric smoker. In my experience charcoal provides better brine penetration.

## Instructions

Rinse scallops, then pat them dry with a towel. Combine all dry ingredients and coat scallops. Place in a bowl, cover and refrigerate for 2 hours. Rinse scallops lightly and pat dry once more. Place scallops on preheated smoker (200° F) with smoldering wood chips for 20 minutes. Remove and set aside. Preheat sauté pan with oil. Season scallops with salt and pepper. Sear 1 to 2 minutes per side and serve hot. This goes well with the Curried Beurre Blanc sauce (see recipe page 141).

# Ceviche Superior

Serves 6
Prep Time: 1 hour
Cook Time: 24 hours to brine

## Ingredients

1/2 pound fresh lake trout fillets
1/2 pound fresh whitefish fillets
3/4 cup fresh lime juice
1/4 cup fresh lemon juice
1/2 teaspoon salt
1/4 cup onion, chopped
1/4 cup green bell pepper, chopped
2 Tablespoons fresh dill weed, minced
1/2 teaspoon fresh garlic, minced
1/4 teaspoon cracked pepper (or 3-4 drops hot pepper sauce)

> **Chef's tip:** For a real treat, serve garnished with American Golden, our local style of caviar.

## Instructions

Skin trout and whitefish and cut into bite-sized pieces. In a glass or stainless steel bowl, combine fish with lime and lemon juice and salt. Stir until salt is dissolved. Add the rest of the ingredients and stir to mix well. Cover and refrigerate for 24 hours, stirring several times. Remove from brine and serve with artisan crackers. May be stored tightly covered in the refrigerator for several days.

## Freshwater Shrimp

One regular guest was a big fan of Mom's cooking and often popped into the kitchen to thank her. One night, he asked if she'd ever served "freshwater shrimp." She'd never heard of them.

"Well," he said, "you might know them as crawfish."

Mary had seen crawfish, but most were smaller than her thumb. She asked, "How would I clean them?"

The guest assured her that he could procure freshwater shrimp as large as any of the jumbo prawns she'd served. His family had trapped them for generations and he offered to bring some.

Not many days later, he showed up with a huge banana box of large crawfish. Much to Mary's surprise, they were alive and squirming. (Mom pretends everything grows on a tree, even leg of lamb.) She accepted the gift, but once he'd gone, she asked a waiter to take the little critters away.

The next morning at 6 a.m., Mom came to start breakfast. Suddenly, her piercing screams were heard all over the house. Dad and I ran down to the kitchen, where we found Mom on top of the refrigerator (to this day we have no idea how she got up there). Scuttling across the floor heading right for her was a giant freshwater shrimp! A true survivor, he had crawled out of the box to get his revenge. Perhaps Mom should have cooked them after all. ⌇

# Roasted Eggplant Spread
## on Toasted Pita

Yields 24 pieces
Prep Time: 10 minutes
Cook Time: 50 minutes

## Ingredients

1 eggplant, peeled
2 red bell peppers, seeded
1 red onion, peeled
2 cloves garlic, minced
3 Tablespoons olive oil
1-1/2 teaspoons kosher salt
1-1/2 teaspoons black pepper, freshly ground
2 Tablespoons tomato paste
4 pita rounds

## Instructions

Preheat oven to 400° F. Cut the eggplant, bell
pepper and onion into 1-inch cubes. Toss
vegetables in a large bowl with the garlic, olive
oil, salt and pepper.

Spread prepared vegetables on a baking sheet and roast
for 45 minutes until they are lightly browned and soft, tossing once during cooking. Cool
slightly.

Place the vegetables in a food processor fitted with a steel blade. Add the tomato paste and
pulse 3 or 4 times to blend. Taste and add salt and pepper as needed.

Cut stack of 4 pitas into 6 wedges, placing them on a baking sheet. Spread 2 tablespoons
of the mix on each pita wedge. Bake in a 350° F oven for 3 minutes before serving.

# Cumin-Spiced Crab Cakes

Yields 8 cakes
Prep Time: 40 minutes
Cook Time: 10 minutes

## Ingredients

**For crab cakes**

12 ounces cooked crab, chunked
1/4 cup red pepper, finely diced
1/4 cup red onion, finely diced
1/4 cup celery, finely diced
2 Tablespoons olive oil
1 Tablespoon garlic, minced
1 Tablespoon lemon juice
2 Tablespoons cumin
2 teaspoons salt
1/2 teaspoon pepper
1/2 cup mayonnaise
1-1/2 cup panko bread crumbs
2 quarts vegetable oil for frying

**For breading**

1 cup all-purpose flour, seasoned with salt and pepper
6 eggs, beaten well
2 cups panko bread crumbs

| |
|---|
| **Chef's tip:** I like to serve these with a mango purée on the side. |

## Instructions

Preheat vegetable oil to 325° F in a deep pan, suitable for frying. Combine vegetables, salt and pepper, garlic and 2 tablespoons of oil in separate sauté pan. Cook until onions are translucent (about 5 minutes). Set aside to cool. Combine veggies, crab, lemon juice, cumin, salt, pepper, mayo and panko. Shape into 2-inch discs and refrigerate. Place panko, flour and eggs into three separate bowls and bread the crab cakes in the following order: flour, eggs and panko. Fry until golden brown (2-4 minutes).

# Fried Whitefish Livers

This is definitely a local dish and the livers are sold only at Bodin Fisheries in town. They are packaged frozen as well as fresh, so bring a cooler on your next visit to take some home. There simply is no substitute for this local product to purchase, though if you fish, you can save the livers from other species. I have used walleye livers, for example.

Serves 4
Prep Time: 15 minutes
Cook Time: 10 minutes

## Ingredients

12 ounces whitefish livers
1/2 cup all-purpose flour, seasoned with salt and pepper
2 cups canola oil for frying
1 red pepper, julienned
1 small red onion, julienned
1 cup crimini mushrooms, sliced
1 teaspoon garlic, minced
2 Tablespoons butter
1/4 cup crispy bacon, chopped (optional garnish)

**Chef's tip:** Make sure to rinse the livers thoroughly before frying to eliminate any "fishy" flavor.

## Instructions

Preheat oil to 325° F in a pan suitable for frying. In a separate pan, sauté peppers, onions, mushrooms and garlic in butter. Dredge livers in flour and fry in hot oil for about 3 minutes. Serve over veggies with Horseradish Cream Sauce (see recipe next page). For a real treat, garnish with chopped bacon bits.

**Mary's Horseradish Cream Sauce**

3 cups mayonnaise
1/2 cup fresh-squeezed lemon juice
1/4 cup prepared horseradish
1/4 cup ketchup
1 Tablespoon paprika
2 Tablespoons fresh parsley, chopped
2 Tablespoons fresh dill, chopped
1 teaspoon fresh garlic, minced

Combine ingredients and let rest until livers
cook. Serve as a side condiment.

> **Chef's tip:** Or try a mayo-free alternative:
> 1/2 cup sour cream
> 1/4 cup horseradish
> 1 teaspoon garlic, minced
> 1 Tablespoon lemon juice
> salt and pepper to taste
> 1/2 Tablespoon of paprika (optional)

# Whitefish Liver Paté

Lest you think our local whitefish livers are not versatile, here is another tasty recipe.

Serves 6
Prep Time: 30 minutes
Cook Time: 4 hours (chilling) plus 30 minutes (at room temperature)

## Ingredients

2 pounds whitefish livers, rinsed, drained and patted dry
   (trout, cod or sole livers may be substituted)
6 Tablespoons butter
2 cloves garlic
1 teaspoon salt
1/2 teaspoon black pepper, ground
1/4 teaspoon allspice, ground
1/2 teaspoon nutmeg, ground
2 Tablespoons cognac
1 teaspoon lemon juice

> **Chef's tip:** This recipe also works well
> with chicken livers as a substitute.

## Instructions

Heat butter in a skillet until it bubbles. Sauté livers over medium heat until brown on
the outside. Remove from heat. Drain off excess butter. Combine garlic, seasonings,
cognac, lemon juice and livers in a food processor fitted with a steel blade. Process
until smooth and creamy. Transfer pâté to a crock. Cover and refrigerate at least 4
hours. Let stand 30 minutes at room temperature before serving.

# Our Town

## A Bit About Bayfield

So who are the 487 or so people who live in Bayfield?

They are the first people, descendants of the Ojibwe people who came to Madeline Island hundreds of years ago and settled also on the mainland. There are descendants of French fur-trading voyageurs from the 1700s and 1800s, and from loggers who clear-cut the Peninsula around the turn of the 20th century.

More recently, they are those visitors like our family, who came for the weekend, and ultimately couldn't bear to leave and found ways to return and stay.

Almost everyone who lives in Bayfield seems to do so by choice. I recall my father once asking his friend Marjorie Benton, "Have you lived in Bayfield *all* your life?"

"No," she cheerfully replied. "Not yet!"

A New England-style village founded in 1856, Bayfield was built on a hillside overlooking Lake Superior and a protected natural harbor framed by the Apostle Islands chain. The city has seen boom and bust cycles with lumbering and fishing as well as the very short-lived brownstone quarrying there. Early on it attracted tourists thanks to

*William Cronon*

its beautiful setting and fresh, relatively pollen-free air.

Two major influences on the city's early growth were the opening of the Soo Locks to large, western-traveling vessels in 1855 – the year before the city was established – and then the arrival of the Chicago/St. Paul/Minneapolis and Omaha Railroad in 1883. The founding of Duluth and Superior as the far western ports, plus declines in available lumber and in Lake Superior fish populations contributed to a reduction from Bayfield's heydays.

The Bayfield High School band marches by Old Rittenhouse Inn (top) while Mayor Larry MacDonald (bottom) soaks up attention at the Apple Fest parade. An eagle-eye view (facing page) shows why Bayfield is a great launching point to the Apostle Islands National Lakeshore.

Bayfield is the mainland gateway to the Apostle Islands archipelago – 21 of the islands are part of the Apostle Islands National Lakeshore and one, Madeline Island, is home to the only year-round island population on this largest freshwater lake in the world.

A favorite destination on Lake Superior, Bayfield was named Best Little Town in the Midwest by the *Chicago Tribune* in 1997 and again in 2007.

Besides its beauty as a draw, there's a lot to do – sailing, kayaking, tour boating, fishing and hiking, not to mention visiting charming shops and galleries and eating great food. It's where you catch the Madeline Island Ferry for the short ride across the bay to scenic Madeline Island. It's also home to a host of wonderful festivals and outdoor activities, a sampling of which I'd like to share with you here.

*Grandon Harris*

Parades, families and lots of apples – could there be a better way to celebrate the harvest? The Bayfield Apple Festival attracts thousands of visitors, some of whom join in the fun. The Pipes and Drums of Thunder Bay (with the banner) always visit the Inn and play for the guests … and it costs us just a few brews for the crew to pay the pipers.

# The Autumnal Draw

For more than 50 autumns, Bayfield has hosted its annual Apple Festival the first full weekend of each October.

For many people, the Bayfield Apple Festival is all they know about our small town. It's considered, I can proudly say, one of the premier fall festivals in the United States.

For those of us who live and work in Bayfield, Apple Fest is a crazy 72-hour rush, when this town of 500 residents swells to 60,000 people, most wandering on or within a few blocks of Rittenhouse Avenue. Every available spot on anybody's lawn becomes a parking spot. There is the parade, the carnival, the vendors with their arts and crafts, music and food (much of it based on the apple). It's a wonderful time of year with the fruits of the orchards on display. Yes, even after decades of Apple Festivals, I still look forward to biting into a fresh caramel apple!

One Apple Festival tradition for us at Old Rittenhouse Inn is a visit by members of the Pipes and Drums of Thunder Bay during our dinner service that Saturday night. Garbed in kilts and other highland attire, they weave through our dining rooms with bagpipes and snare drums in full voice. It's amazing. The guests always levitate, jumping up to give the musicians a spontaneous ovation.

All the musicians ask for is a few rounds of beer, which we're happy to oblige.

Of course, I could not be Mary and Jerry's son without some musical inclinations myself. During Apple Fest, I play with the popular local band Fido and the Love Dogs at the Bayfield Lakeside Pavilion. The Pipes and Drums show up there as well. On occasion, we'll play a song together, but usually they come to do a number or two inside the pavilion while our band takes a break. The Scottish musical rumble gets the crowd amped up.

The weeks before and sometimes after Apple Fest can bring the most spectacular scenes of the year. Around the Bayfield Peninsula and the Apostle Islands, unlike the more boreal forests of Lake Superior's western and northern shores, you'll find numerous oaks and maples that spark the reds and golds of autumn's blaze. Contrasted against that is the brilliant blue of the Big Lake.

The Apple Fest also marks the month of my son's birth and of my own Halloween birthday, making this a fantastic season worth a special toast (with spiced apple cider, of course).

Bayfield in Bloom with 50,000 blooming daffodils planted around town kicks off the spring-summer events.

# One Hopping Town

Although the Bayfield Apple Festival dominates the calendar of events, it seems like almost every week there's something interesting going on in Bayfield and the region.

Bayfield in Bloom kickstarts the spring season from mid-May to mid-June and is a celebration of spring and all things horticultural, with advice from experts, activities for gardeners and a spotlight on the orchards and flower farms. The community's 50,000 blossoming daffodils bring welcome color after a long winter of white. The final event for the celebration comes in June with a Blessing of the Fleet, when local clergy of many denominations bless fishing and recreational vessels as the boats parade by them.

Throughout the summer, people travel from across the region to Lake Superior Big Top Chautauqua. This summer-long festival under the big blue canvas at Mount Ashwabay features original musical histories and concerts by regional and national artists like Greg Brown, Trampled by Turtles, Lyle Lovett, Bonnie Raitt and Willie Nelson.

The Bayfield Festival of Arts the third weekend in July is more than 50 years old. It pulls in large numbers of people to Memorial Park on the waterfront to leisurely check out the pottery, jewelry, painting, photography and other artwork. During the festival weekend, galleries offer open houses, demonstrations and sales.

The Fall Harvest Celebration runs through September and October and includes the annual Apple Festival. It's a great time to tour Bayfield's apple orchards and fruit farms, which are easy to reach along the hilltop above town. And you'll find that the owners love to chat with visitors.

*Grandon Harris*

The diversity of activities in the area is amazing. From top are: The annual Blessing of the Fleet near the Bayfield Pavilion; two shots from the Lake Superior Big Top Chautauqua; dancers in jingle dresses at a local Ojibwe pow wow; the barn at Hauser's Superior View Farm with flowers for Bayfield in Bloom; one of several bicycle trails through the woods (one links Bayfield with Washburn).

*Jeff Wenz*

Beautiful scenery and recreation abound. From the top: the marina at sunset; end of day at the beach; Apostle Highlands Golf Course; the Brownstone Trail that starts downtown; and the lighthouse on Sand Island, part of the Apostle Islands National Lakeshore.

# The Apostles & Madeline Island

The Apostle Islands are a true gem of our region. Apostle Islands National Lakeshore encompasses 21 islands and 2,500 acres of the Bayfield Peninsula mainland.

It's one of only four national lakeshores in the country (Pictured Rocks in Michigan is also on Lake Superior, Sleeping Bear Dunes in Michigan and Indiana Dunes in Indiana are both on Lake Michigan). The Apostle Islands are popular for boating, sailing, paddling and sightseeing. Apostle Islands Cruises are a comfortable option for visiting the islands, with scenic, narrated excursions departing from downtown Bayfield.

The Apostle Islands National Lakeshore Visitor Center in the Old Bayfield County Courthouse on Washington Avenue has information, a lighthouse exhibit, a bookstore and a 20-minute film, "On the Edge of Gichigami – Voices of the Apostle Islands." My parents got involved in saving the old courthouse building, and it is worth a visit.

More than 50 miles of trails are maintained in the lakeshore, and you can camp on 18 of the 21 islands. In the Apostles are numerous shipwreck sites, some visible from the surface under the right conditions. The perfect excuse to see some of the eight lighthouses or towers on the islands is the annual Apostle Islands Lighthouse Celebration in September.

# Sea Caves

In 2014, the phenomenon we call the "ice caves" drew 120,000 unexpected visitors to the Bayfield Peninsula from mid-January until mid-March when the National Park Service closed the official access to the caves.

*Bill Hooper*

The sea caves are accessible by kayak or boat in summer, and some occasionally by foot in winter.

*Phil Bencomo*

*Phil Bencomo*

Winter transforms the sea caves with ice and makes many of them accessible by a long walk on the lake.

It was reported by social media and national news outlets that the ice caves were accessible from the mainland for the first time in five years. Travelers poured in from around the country and the world to see what has become a rare occurrence. The opportunity to see the caves in winter garb is rare because Lake Superior had not been freezing adequately to allow safe walking on the ice.

But in 2014, the caves were open for business, which meant our area restaurants and lodgings suddenly had to gear up for summer-sized crowds. As many as 20,000 visitors to the caves (and the area) were recorded on weekends when we usually have our "quiet" time.

My wife Wendy was among the very first to break trail on the ice caves that winter. She was trying out her photo skills with a digital camera – technology that creates opportunity for fantastic images. It's a good thing she visited early. Once the crowds started arriving, we buckled down with a small seasonal staff to keep food on the table at the Landmark Restaurant and the rooms clean at Old Rittenhouse Inn and Le Château.

The ice caves are actually the iced-over sea caves that time and Lake Superior have worn into the sandstone cliffs, mainly on the north shore of Devils Island, at Swallow Point on Sand Island and along the western mainland of the Apostle Islands National Lakeshore.

That winter the lakeshore ended up as busy as peak season. The Park Service called for help from parks around the country to direct traffic and handle the crowds taking the 3-mile round-trip trek from mainland to the caves. We managed to happily weather the unexpected gift that an icy cold winter (and the power of social media and news reporting) gave us.

# Ice Road

Jerry loves to tell this story: "When Mary was at the front desk in the winter, people would come up and ask her about the ice road to Madeline Island. 'Do they drive across the ice?' they'd ask. Mary would lean close to them and say, 'Yes … *THEY* do.'"

Trees line the edge of the temporary road.

Mary herself, you see, would never travel across that ice road for anything. It's hard to blame her; that road is always iffy.

What, you might wonder, is an ice road?

First you need to know that Madeline Island has residents: Almost 2,500 live there during the open-water seasons of summer and fall, but only about 300 reside on the island all year. After fifth grade, children on the island must come to the mainland for school. Many of the year-round residents also come across for work. They traverse the almost 4 miles of water daily or weekly – whether it's open water, semi-frozen or thick ice cover. La Pointe is the only town on the island and there is a wonderful museum, a marina, restaurants, lodgings and other amenities there. It's the ferry stop, too.

The Madeline Island Ferry Line operates four ferries, with the last boat heading to the island at 5:30 p.m. (winter hours), 8:30 p.m. (off-season) or 10 p.m. (peak tourism season). Islanders with their own boats can make the crossing on their own in summer or fall. In early winter and early spring, when conditions churn up a mix of ice and open water, Windsled Transportation takes over with its versatile windsleds. But the drawback for islanders is that it's home by 4:30 p.m. to catch the last ride.

The most liberating transportation time of the year is deep winter, when the ice has frozen to a reasonable thickness and a temporary ice road is plotted. The builders of this winter wonder line the "road" with used Christmas trees, which keep you on the path and prevent you from getting lost in a blizzard. The trees are a good solution, since the road rarely opens by Christmas.

The opening of the ice road is the only time of the year that "Islanders" are not at the mercy of someone else's schedule; they can come and go as they please, as long as the ice holds them. Before the ice road opens in winter, if your child is involved in an evening sports event or if you want to catch a play at the local theater, you either spend the night at a hotel or a friend's house, or you don't get to go.

That's why Islanders are so crazy about the ice road and will drive on it even with 6 inches of standing water on top. Some people do go through that ice and often those people are locals – they are the first, and last, ones to tempt fate each year.

At times there are huge cracks in the ice. Sometimes people build bridges over these pressure cracks or "heaves." Another technique to keep the ice road usable is to chip and file down the area around a pressure crack, filling it with an icy slurry to repair or smooth the crack. Sometimes Lake Superior's open water may be just a half-mile away from the road, but still some will travel.

One of the first times I traveled on the ice road was at age 17 when my best friend, Dan, came with some friends from Hayward. They visited the first week in April. He was driving his mother's old custard-colored Crown Victoria. A former cop car, the back windows were locked shut and the back doors couldn't be opened from the inside. Not the kind of car you can exit fast, if you get my drift.

Seven of us piled into the Crown Vic and decided to drive to Madeline Island. We weren't deterred by the 8 inches of water on top of the ice. It was a beautiful sunny day, but still rather cold, and we saw other cars going so we figured it was safe. Safe enough, anyway.

We drove out from the city beach onto the ice, going quite fast. Dan gunned it the whole way as we howled and laughed. Sometimes he'd twirl the wheel and slam the brakes at the same time and we'd spin 360 degrees, wildly throwing giant rooster tails of icy water 30 feet in the air.

We got to the island and drove around a bit, but didn't turn toward home until dusk. Looking back across to the mainland, the watery ice suddenly seemed very scary. Mary's ice-road wisdom was sinking into me.

The fading sunlight glowed on the giant pool of water in front of us. Not knowing if there were holes or weak spots, we set off with trepidation. Dan did what any reasonable teenager would do – he gunned the car as fast as it would go despite the drag of the water on the wheels and the rooster tail shooting up behind us. We did maybe 50 to 60 miles an hour for the longest three minutes of my life. We were silent the whole way, exhaling only when we reached the mainland. We were a really lucky dumb bunch of kids, but it was one of the greatest thrills any of us had ever had.

*Gary Knowles*
John & Mary Thiel run dog teams as Wolfsong, offering dogsled adventures on ice and snow.

# It Seemed Like a Good Idea

Some guests were enjoying a late-morning breakfast in March 1977 when they noticed something large moving slowly across the frozen Lake Superior. Just as they asked, "What on earth is that?" the thing broke through the ice and started to sink. The guests screamed, and we, of course, came running, not knowing what to expect. Relieved nothing was amiss in the dining room, we stayed to watch the whole show.

*Bayfield Chamber & Visitor Bureau*
A warning worth heeding on the ice road.

Someone found a pair of binoculars, and we discovered the bulky thing was a house sinking slowly through the ice. We didn't see any sign of the truck that must have been hauling it. The water there could be 75 to 100 feet, but the house didn't sink to the bottom. The wood construction and decent insulation made it buoyant enough that it settled with the top 5 feet still showing above the surface.

Later, we learned more of the story. The house was one of three built as "spec homes" that never sold. A fellow got a good deal on all three houses because they had to be moved. He bought land on Madeline Island and decided to drive them over one by one to become seasonal homes. This had been the first one. Most believe that March 2 was way too late in the year for such a heavy load on the ice road. Another mistake was going too far around the southern channel of Mad Isle, which is notorious for its currents and risky ice.

Big wheels on a trailer, plus a heavy truck, equalled too much weight. I think he might have made it if he'd have gone faster, but at a slow pace, the wet ice cracked, the back wheel went in and that was that. The driver got out okay.

The Wisconsin DNR was not happy with the half-floating house. The order came to pull it out or sink it. Workers sandbagged the building – with all of the furnishings – and sunk it into the 75 feet of water for the remainder of winter.

In spring, the owner sent a crane, and divers went down with cables to attach to the structure. They hoped to get the roof in one piece, but the whole house just ripped all apart, sprinkling the refrigerator, stove, rugs and Laura Ashley furnishings to the bottom of the lake. Thankfully, the truck was recovered.

# Soups

# Curried Broccoli Soup

This is one of my mom's soups from the early days of the restaurant. It is one dish that I can literally taste (in my mind) any time I think of it. Delish!

Serves 6-8
Prep Time: 15 minutes
Cook Time: 45 minutes

## Ingredients

1-1/2 pounds broccoli (3 average stalks)
2 cups chicken stock or broth
3-4 cloves garlic, minced
1/4 cup green onions, minced, tops included
1/2 teaspoon nutmeg
3/4 teaspoon curry
1 cup heavy cream

## Instructions

In large saucepan, cook broccoli in stock until tender. Place broccoli into a blender and purée it using the hot stock. Return mixture to saucepan and simmer with other ingredients on low heat, about 20 minutes. Serve warm in soup bowls. Some ideas for garnishing this dish include broccoli florets, toasted croutons, or fresh dill and nova lox (pictured above).

# Lake Superior Chowder

This is a signature dish for the Landmark Restaurant at Old Rittenhouse Inn. It's almost always on the menu and features two local favorites – trout and whitefish – plus clam stock to give it great flavor. We offer this during every Apple Festival weekend and serve about 20 gallons a day.

Serves 6-8
Prep Time: 30 minutes
Cook Time: 45 minutes

## Ingredients

1 small onion, diced
4 stalks celery, diced
1 carrot, diced
1 teaspoon salt
1 teaspoon pepper
1 Tablespoon fresh garlic, minced
3 Tablespoons olive oil
1 cup white wine
4 cups vegetable stock
1 can clams in juice (16 ounces)
8 ounces fresh lake trout,
    boneless fillets
2 cups Yukon gold potatoes, diced
    to 1/2-inch cubes, skins on
8 ounces fresh whitefish,
    boneless fillets
3 sprigs basil
2 bay leaves
2 sprigs thyme
4 Tablespoons butter, melted
1/3 cups flour
1 cup heavy cream

## Instructions

In a 4-quart, heavy-bottom pan, sauté onion, celery, carrot, salt and pepper, garlic and oil for about 5 minutes. Add wine and reduce by half. Add vegetable stock, clams and their juice. Bring to boil, then add fish fillets and potatoes. Simmer on medium-low for about 10 minutes. Add herbs and bay leaves and simmer for another 10 minutes. Mix butter and flour to make a roux, adding to chowder to thicken. Finish with heavy cream. Sliced green onions, soaked in cold water to curl them, make a nice garnish.

# Fire-Roasted Red Pepper & Crab Bisque

Serves 4-6
Prep Time: 1 hour
Cook Time: 30 minutes

## Ingredients

4 red peppers, halved and seeded
3 cups chicken stock
1 onion, diced
1 Tablespoon fresh garlic, minced
2 Tablespoons canola oil
1 cup white wine
1 king crab, cooked and shelled (about 12 ounces)
1 cup heavy cream
1 teaspoon salt
1 teaspoon pepper
6 green onions, sliced for garnish

## Instructions

Preheat gas/charcoal grill. Grill red pepper halves for 10 to 15 minutes. Peel off any charred skin. Place in blender and purée with chicken stock, set aside. Place onions, garlic and oil in 4-quart stock pot and cook on medium for about 5 minutes. Add wine and reduce by half. Add red pepper purée and crab meat, cook on low for about 20 minutes, stirring occasionally. Finish with salt, pepper and cream. Garnish with green onion.

# Heirloom Tomato & Basil Gazpacho

Serves 4-6
Prep Time: 20 minutes
Cook Time: 1 hour 30 minutes

## Ingredients

1 pound heirloom tomatoes
1 small onion, diced
1 Tablespoon fresh garlic, minced
1 Tablespoon olive oil
1 cup Riesling white wine
1 cucumber, peeled, seeded and diced
3 cups vegetable stock
2 Tablespoons honey
4 sprigs basil, julienned
salt for blanching
2 cups ice + 4 cups cold water after blanching

## Instructions

Place 4-quart pot of salted water on medium-high heat to blanch tomatoes. In a large pot, combine ice and water to make an ice bath and set aside. Score tomatoes with an "X" on bottom. When water is boiling, blanch tomatoes for 2 minutes. Strain from water and place in ice bath. Once tomatoes are cooled, peel, seed and dice them and set aside. Place onion, garlic and oil in 4-quart stock pot and sauté for 5 minutes. Add wine and reduce by half. Add vegetable stock, tomatoes, cucumber and honey. Cook on low for about 20 minutes. Remove from heat and finish with basil. Transfer to refrigerator to chill for at least 1 hour before serving.

## Our Backyard Gardens

In the early 1990s, one couple would come to the Inn for dinner whenever they visited Bayfield. Like us, they soon fell in love with the community and eventually bought a summer home. They became "seasonal farmers" for us when they discovered a fantastic feral patch of asparagus on their property. It took time to bring it under control and to peak production, but once they did, we reaped the benefits of high-quality, homegrown asparagus for our menu.

Bayfield has its own local broccoli, too. It's a little taller

# Creamy Wild Leek with Double Smoked Ham Soup

Serves 6-8
Prep Time: 15 minutes
Cook Time: 30 minutes

## Ingredients

1 cup wild leeks, julienned (or use green onions)
1 pound double-smoked ham, diced
1 carrot, diced
3 stalks celery, diced
1 small white onion, diced
1 Tablespoon fresh garlic, minced
2 Tablespoons canola oil
2 teaspoons smoked paprika
3 cups chicken stock
1 cup heavy cream
3 Tablespoons butter, melted
1/4 cup all-purpose flour
salt and pepper to taste

## Instructions

Place carrots, celery, onion, garlic and oil in a 4-quart stock pot and sauté on medium heat for about 5 minutes. Add chicken stock, ham and leeks and cook on medium-low for about 20 minutes, stirring occasionally. While soup is simmering, mix melted butter and flour together to make a roux. Mix roux with soup to thicken. Finish with cream and salt and pepper to taste.

and looser on the bud than store-bought, but what flavor! I love Mom's Curried Broccoli Soup when enhanced with the local stalks and flowerets. Thinking about it brings the flavor indelibly to mind.

The ravines where creeks run through to the Lake, the forested areas north of town and any slightly marshy lowlands are fertile ground for wild harvest of watercress, ramps and fiddlehead ferns.

One can always find something edible and delicious growing in those areas; it's just a matter of knowing where they grow and when. They can literally be found for free for those with training.

At Old Rittenhouse Inn, gardeners tend a nice little herb garden that produces all our chives and basil, a lot of our rosemary and other herbs. Nice heirloom tomatoes grow here, too, and we look forward to late August when we can serve our own tomatoes and basil. Especially with salads, it's easy to experiment using what grows locally. Feel free to experiment using your local harvest and you'll find, like we have, that fresh remains forever the best. ~

# Chicken Amaretto
# with Wild Rice Soup

Serves 8
Prep Time: 40 minutes
Cook Time: 20 minutes

## Ingredients

6 cups chicken stock
1 cup cooked chicken breast, finely chopped
2 cups wild rice, slightly undercooked
1 Tablespoon lemon juice
1/4 teaspoon almond extract or 2 ounces amaretto liqueur
1 cup slivered almonds
1 cup heavy cream
1 cup mild baby swiss cheese, grated
2 teaspoons sliced almonds, toasted

## Instructions

Bring stock to a boil. Reduce heat and simmer gently for five minutes. Add chicken, wild rice, lemon juice and almond extract. Cook about 20 minutes. Just before serving, add slivered almonds and cream. Garnish with grated swiss cheese and toasted almonds.

# Raspberry Gazpacho

Since the early days of our restaurant, we've always enjoyed creating soups that feature the lovely berries grown in this area. My personal favorite is raspberries, with their jewel-like appearance and concentrated flavor. This summer-kissed recipe will have your dinner guests raving.

Serves 4
Prep Time: 20 minutes
Cook Time: 2 hours 30 minutes

# Ingredients

3 cups fresh raspberries
3/4 cup water
2 Tablespoons lemon juice
2 Tablespoons lemon rind, finely grated
2 Tablespoons arrowroot
1/2 cup maple syrup
2 cups sparkling white grape juice
1/2 cup sour cream (or yogurt)
1/2 cup fresh raspberries for garnish

# Instructions

Purée the 3 cups raspberries for soup and strain through a sieve into bowl, then set aside. Take seeds and rind left in sieve and transfer to saucepan. Add water and simmer for 5 minutes. Strain water into bowl containing berry juice and discard any seeds remaining in sieve. Combine lemon juice, lemon rind and arrowroot and add the combination to the berry juice. Add maple syrup and sparkling juice, transfer to saucepan. Simmer over low heat until thick. Refrigerate 2 hours. Serve chilled in individual bowls with a dollop or swirl of sour cream and a spoonful of berries on top of each bowl.

# Harvest Squash Bisque

Serves 4-6
Prep Time: 15 minutes
Cook Time: 1 hour 30 minutes

## Ingredients

1 pound butternut squash
1 pound acorn squash
1 pound sweet potatoes
4 cups vegetable stock
1 small yellow onion, diced
1 Tablespoon garlic
1/4 cup maple syrup
1/4 cup brown sugar
1 teaspoon nutmeg
1/4 cups cream sherry
1/4 teaspoon white pepper
2 cups heavy cream

**Chef's tip:** To avoid burned hands, be sure to use gloves when peeling roasted squash and purée it immediately after peeling.

## Instructions

Preheat oven to 375° F. Cut all squash and sweet potatoes lengthwise and remove seeds with a spoon. Place squash and potatoes in a baking pan and bake about 45 minutes or until cooked through. Place vegetable stock, onion and garlic in stock pot and bring to a boil. Reduce heat and simmer for 10 minutes. After squash and sweet potatoes are done and cooled slightly, peel them. Place in food processor and purée with vegetable stock mixture in two batches. Return purée back to stove and add syrup, brown sugar, cream sherry, nutmeg, white pepper and heavy cream. Simmer on low for 30 minutes.

Paul L. Hayden

# Farmers, Foragers and Friends

## Going Wild

The Bayfield Peninsula, famous for apples, offers so much more for the culinary minded. The regional foods include watercress, fiddlehead ferns, ramps, mushrooms, berries and many orchard fruits, plus delectable trout, whitefish and herring from Lake Superior.

In the Inn's early days, economics, as much as a buy-local philosophy, drove our focus on regional cuisine. Only one truck per week brought supplies from distant wholesale grocers, and Mary grew incredibly adept at ordering just enough for the week's meals … or she'd be stuck with wasted food.

So Mary welcomed the pantry supplements brought by local producers and foragers. Fresh fish, of course, were usually plentiful, and Mary would visit the farmer's market down the street to buy the best of whatever was available.

The woods and fields yield a variety, too, of non-cultivated, wild produce. My spring seasonal favorite is morel mushrooms sautéed in fresh salty butter. They put the mmmm in mushroommmmm. Or maybe I prefer the wild strawberries, raspberries and blueberries. It's so hard to pick a favorite, and here I can have them all.

While on occasion we'll head to the fields ourselves, most of this wild cornucopia comes to us thanks to seasonal foragers. We've met a few endearing characters from these exchanges. Certain ones pop into my mind whenever I think of these foods we love.

## The Blueberry Boys

Ed and Alec were Mary's "Blueberry Boys." I don't recall their last names, or even if I ever knew them, but I can see their faces clearly in my mind – two adorable little old men with lined faces and clear, shiny eyes. They wore those little hats with the flaps over the ears à la Stormy Kromer, flannel jackets over baggy, colorless pants, and old leather boots – in short, the Scandinavian bachelor farmer uniform.

They were small of stature, and just a joy to be around, even though they both had a look about them that said, "I know the secret, but I'm not telling." (That would be the location of the wild blueberry patches.)

Even in their most chatty moments, Ed talked little and Alec not so much. They eventually warmed up, accepting Mary's repeated invitations to stay for coffee and muffins.

Every year when the wild blueberries ripened, that became our tradition. Ed and Alec would show up with these tiny, tasty jewels – the "caviar of the forest," as my dad called them. Mary bought everything they had, which was only fair, we joked, since Ed and Alec competed against black bears for the berries. It was worth the effort. If you've ever sampled wild blueberries side by side with cultivated blueberries, you know that the smaller berries burst with bigger taste.

After making their sale, Ed and Alec would sit with Mary and the waitresses, teasing a bit, flirting a little, always in good fun. The Blueberry Boys sat at "K1" – a kitchen table that is long gone now, as are the "boys." They would devour the muffins Mary had left from breakfast. They learned to like our "strong" coffee, too. (I suspect they stretched their own brew out by watering it down.) Their mischievous grins became one of our annual signs of the harvest season.

# The Mushroom Man

One forager who supplies us with the region's wild bounty stands out as exceptional. Marvin Defoe – The Mushroom Man – shows up with these sensational mushrooms throughout the changing 'shroom seasons. You never quite know what he has until you see what is in the box – wild morels, chanterelles, black trumpet mushrooms, chicken of the woods, lobster mushrooms or maybe giant puffballs.

The variety has taught us the different flavors and varying textures. Harvesting wild mushrooms, the edible kind, can be tricky business and not for the uninformed, but Marvin knows his stuff.

The most amazing to me are the puffballs that grow right in the ravine next to the Inn. Now if you told me as a kid that it's good to eat a puffball, I would have told you to fly a kite or take a hike or something equally dismissive. Not all puffballs are edible, but these massive marvels are among the best-tasting mushrooms, plus they have a pleasing texture and delicate white flesh. They are superb and complement so many sauces, accent sautés or side dishes. They make our vegan customers very happy.

Marvin leaves hysterically funny messages in the ebbing hours of the night. We thrill to hear these communications because we know to expect The Mushroom Man with a culinary treasure later that day.

# The Farm Harvest

Jutting into Lake Superior, the Bayfield Peninsula often reaps the benefits of what we call "lake effect" snows. We may curse this aspect of local living while shoveling in winter, but for our area farms, the consistent ground cover protects, and later nourishes, soil and plants. The lake, a giant heat absorber, also slows most fall frosts. An agricultural gift to this region came from the glaciers – a rich, sandy soil in contrast to the hard clays in other areas around the lake.

Thanks to these gifts, the hills surrounding our town support orchards. Bayfield's famous Apple Festival has been around more than 50 years, and the orchards were here several generations before that.

There are so many great family farms and orchards that I almost hesitate to highlight just a few. Their quality produce helps us to get the rave reviews we often enjoy for the Landmark Restaurant's menu.

We partner with the farms in other ways, too, often taking the motorcoach groups that dine at the restaurant "up the hill" to visit the orchards in summer and fall.

One of the most scenic properties is Blue Vista Farm. Its well-maintained, century-old barn features fieldstone construction and impressive timber beams. The surrounding farm and yard offer breathtaking views of Lake Superior and overlook Mount Ashwabay, home to Lake Superior Big Top Chautauqua with its under-the-blue-canvas concerts and performances. Husband and wife owners of Blue Vista, Eric Carlson and Ellen Kwiatkowski, cultivate 6 acres of blueberries, 5 acres of raspberries, 2 acres of flowers, and more than 1,500 apple trees. Blue Vista Farm earned its Midwest Organic Services

Most famous for apples, the region also produces cherries, like these from the Apple Hill Orchard (top left). Jim Erickson at the James Erickson Orchard (top right) and a couple of visitors posing at the Blue Vista Farm, are all proudly showing off boxes of some fine blueberries, raspberries and strawberries.

*Jeanne Wiest*

*Cy Dodson*

Association certification and was one of the first farms in the area to be placed in land stewardship, ensuring it will remain farmland forever. The couple's stewardship philosophy is outlined on the farm's website: "Because we firmly believe that small farms and locally produced food are critical for the ecological, economic, and personal health and viability of our communities, we have sold the development rights to our farm to the Bayfield Regional Conservancy and the Town of Bayfield, resulting in a place that is permanently protected from development. Blue Vista Farm will always be a farm."

We also love the James Erickson Orchard & Country Store. Jim and Muriel Erickson have been married for about 60 years, as long as they've owned the orchard. Besides savory apples and homemade apple cider, the orchard has a neat gift shop on-site, where Muriel sells her apple cider doughnuts. People far and wide rave about these apple doughnuts, sprinkled with cinnamon sugar. Eat one, and you'll be hard pressed to keep from devouring a whole bag.

Hauser's Superior View Farm, another hilltop orchard, also grows annual and perennial flowers that are shipped around the country, with apples and berries for sale later in the year. The farm's colorful springtime garden sales offer a wide variety of plants, including the most popular perennials – lilies, delphinium, astilbe and bleeding hearts. They sell berry plants, fruit trees and shrubs. The sale goes on in their 1928 red barn, ordered from the Sears, Roebuck & Company catalog. The Hauser family, with ties to Switzerland, traces its local history back to 1908 when Great-Grandpa John Hauser, a horticulturalist with a knack for raising strawberries and potatoes, arrived in Bayfield. Grandfather J. Dawson Hauser added the apple orchard during

A view through the apple blossoms at the century-old barn at Blue Vista Farms and of the blossoms themselves (facing page).

the Great Depression. The farm passed down to Jim and Marilyn Hauser, and now to Jim Jr. and Ellen. The fifth generation, Dane Hauser has started to work on the farm, too.

The Dale family has operated Highland Valley Farm for more than 35 years and has taken cultivation to an art form in raising organic blueberries, red raspberries and red and black currants. The family – Rick, Janet, Jon, Chris and Magdalen – produces maple syrup from a 12-acre sugar bush operation and makes delightful honey from bees that collect a blend of nectars from raspberry and wildflower blossoms. This honey has a distinctive fruity flavor and aroma that is uniquely Bayfield.

My favorite place for caramel apples is Apple Hill Orchard, which also is known for sweet cherries in July, as well as apples, pears and plums in September. Claudia Ferraro just happens to make the greatest caramel apples I have ever tasted. I especially love the thick caramel she uses, and the cashews or peanuts pressed into it. They also make M&M-pressed apples and other types of candies and cookie coatings, but I love the nuts (don't know what that says about me). You can get these at the farm or at the Bayfield Apple Festival.

These are a mere few of our regional farms and orchards, which number more than a dozen just around Bayfield. While all are unique, they share a few common traits: a love of the land, and working in partnership with the land to feed people. They are artisans whose medium is seeds, dirt, water and sun. The end result, be it the perfect haricot vert green bean or a beautiful little spaghetti squash, is a product of the toil, care and commitment of generations.

# Fresh Fish, Best Fish

Older even than farming in the Bayfield area is the commercial fishing industry, which actually started at the time of the fur traders, who shipped salted fish to the East Coast as another revenue source.

As with farming, today's commercial fishing operations tend to span generations and go by the family names like Bodin, Everett, Halvorson and Peterson. When we first arrived in the 1970s, Lake Superior fishing had declined due to the entrance of the sea lamprey through the St. Lawrence Seaway as well as from overfishing. Since then, thanks to good management, fish stocking programs and sea lamprey controls, the fishing is really coming back and is becoming world-class.

*Wisconsin DNR*

Local commercial operations like Bodin Fisheries bring the freshest catches to the table.

You can see the fishing tugs go off in the early morning, and these days, there's almost always a bounty of great catch for the restaurant. It's no wonder guests so enjoy our local fish dishes. For non-locals, perhaps the oddest thing we serve is sautéed or fried whitefish livers with peppers, onions, mushrooms, bacon and horseradish crème.

The Lake Superior fishery is one of our greatest local resources. Lake trout, whitefish and herring (or cisco or bluefin, if you prefer) are the only fish commercially harvested, but the lake provides many meals to locals and visitors.

For commercial fishing families, this is a way of life. For other residents and visitors, fishing is recreation and Lake Superior or our inland waters offer excellent angling for walleye, smallmouth bass, rainbow trout, sturgeon, pike and perch. The salmon fishery is incredible for the chinook and the steelheads and coho. You've just got to get up here if you like to fish!

# Sixth Street Market

The Inn's commitment to offering local items on the menu has created a partnership with Sixth Street Market in Ashland where we get some of our quality, fresh meats. For 30 years, three generations of the Pearson family have produced tasty sausages and award-winning bratwursts along with great cuts of locally produced beef and pork.

The market reminds me of an old-time butcher shop. It all began with Carl Pearson, who started his meat business in Minnesota after returning from service in World War II. His son and daughter-in-law, Jerry and Linda, later purchased the business in Ashland. Their son, Andy, recently earned certification from UW-Madison as a Master Meat Crafter.

The first Sixth Street Market product we discovered was a double-smoked ham. It was featured with a side of au gratin potatoes for Easter brunch. After trying it, one of the staff said, "This is so fantastic, we should have it on the menu all the time."

So we replaced our breakfast ham with the market's version and have since added their maple cinnamon sausages – tasty links about three times the size you'd expect. They are made with real Wisconsin maple syrup and freshly ground cinnamon. Our breakfast menu also features their thick-sliced smoked bacon, the kind packed with smoky flavor and very little fat once it's cooked. Guests rave about our breakfast meats – proof of

A local artist did a painting reflecting the community feeling of the Sixth Street Market.

Some of the Sixth Street Market crew posing in the store are, from left, Jerry Pearson, Andy Pearson, Steven Kohl and Ryan Olson.

a good decision to incorporate their products.

About five years ago, the Inn began purchasing Jerry Pearson's brats to feature with apple kraut during Apple Festival. Always perfecting his craft, Jerry's brats won the Wisconsin Association of Meat Producers Grand Champion Award in 2013. It's no wonder they always sell out!

In addition to the fresh meats and charcuterie, this small neighborhood market offers an impressive list of locally made products: breads from Ashland Baking Company (Ashland), ice cream from Tetzner's Dairy (Washburn), coffee from Big Water Coffee Roasters (Bayfield) and Northwestern Coffee Mills (Mason), smoked fish from Everett Fisheries (Port Wing), jams and jellies from the Bayfield Apple Company and Hauser's Superior View Farm (both Bayfield), and a variety of Wisconsin cheeses. The market's inventory speaks to the consumers' commitment to buying local foods as well as the richness of foods produced in the area surrounding Chequamegon Bay.

# Salads

# Romaine Salad
## with Sherry Vinaigrette

Serves 12
Prep Time: 15 minutes
Cook Time: 5 minutes

## Ingredients

2 heads Romaine lettuce
1 red onion, chopped
1 cup grape tomatoes
1-1/2 cups Chili-Roasted Almonds with Cranberries (see recipe below)
1-1/2 cups Sherry Vinaigrette (see recipe next page)
1-1/2 cups goat cheese (about 2 Tablespoons per salad)

## Instructions

Toss romaine, onion, tomatoes and vinaigrette. Arrange greens on a chilled plate and top with spiced almond and cranberry mix and crumbled goat cheese.

---

### Chili-Roasted Almonds with Cranberries

1 Tablespoon unsalted butter, melted
1/2 cup raw almonds, sliced
1 teaspoon mild chili powder
1/2 teaspoon ground cumin
1/4 teaspoon salt
1/4 teaspoon dried oregano
1/4 teaspoon cayenne pepper
1/2 cup dried cranberries

Coat raw almonds with the melted butter and spread them evenly on a large sheet pan. Lightly toast the nuts in a 300° to 325° F oven for about 10 minutes, occasionally shaking the pan. Meanwhile, mix together the dry ingredients. When finished toasting, transfer almonds into a large bowl and coat with dry ingredients. Mix in the cranberries until uniformly blended. Cover and store at room temperature.

# Sherry Vinaigrette

## Ingredients

1/4 cup white wine vinegar
1/2 cup sherry
1 Tablespoon lemon juice
1 teaspoon salt
1/4 teaspoon ground pepper
2 Tablespoons Dijon mustard
1/2 cup vegetable oil
1 cup olive oil
1/4 cup fresh herbs (thyme and basil recommended)

> **Chef's tip:** This recipe makes enough dressing for about 24 salads. If you want only enough for a small gathering, cut the portions in half or keep the extra in the refrigerator for up to 10 days.

## Instructions

In a blender, place vinegar, sherry, lemon juice, salt, pepper and Dijon mustard. While blender is running, slowly add the vegetable oil to emulsify. Then quickly add the olive oil and herbs. Take care not to overblend, as the olive oil will become bitter.

# Mixed Baby Greens
## with White Wine Peach Vinaigrette

Serves 4-6
Prep Time: 20 minutes
Cook Time: 5 minutes

## Ingredients

1 pound mixed baby greens
pinch salt & pepper
4 ounces bleu cheese
8 ounces sun-dried calamyrna or black mission figs, julienned
4 ounces roasted pecans
1/2 cup White Wine Peach Vinaigrette (see recipe below)

## Instructions

Combine greens, salt, pepper and vinaigrette in mixing bowl and toss. Top with bleu cheese, figs, and pecans. A strawberry or other fresh fruit adds a nice garnish, too.

---

**White Wine Peach Vinaigrette**
1 fresh peach, skin off, pitted and diced
1/4 cup dry white wine
1/2 cup white wine vinegar
2 Tablespoons honey
pinch salt
1-1/2 cups olive oil

**Chef's tip:** Be sure to add only a few drops of oil at first to start the emulsion. If not, your vinaigrette will "break" (this means the oil and vinegar will not combine and you will have to shake before every use).

Combine wine and peach in saucepan and cook over medium heat until wine is reduced by 80 percent. Transfer peach mix to blender along with the rest of the ingredients except oil. Turn blender on and pour oil in a slow and steady stream.

# Lemon Vinaigrette

Serves 12-14

## Ingredients

3/4 cup lemon juice
1/4 cup white wine vinegar
1 teaspoon Dijon mustard
1/2 teaspoon salt
1 t fresh garlic, minced
2 Tablespoons honey
1-1/2 cups canola oil
1-1/2 cups olive oil

## Instructions

Combine all ingredients in a blender, except the oils. Start blender, adding only a few drops of oil to start to begin the emulsion. Then continue adding oil in a very slow, steady stream until fully incorporated.

## Changing Trout Mid-Theme

Since Mary started using smoked trout in her salads, patés, croquettes and other dishes years ago, it has become a favorite ingredient of our chefs and our guests.

Mary's Smoked Trout Salad (the classic recipe) begins with a bed of leaf lettuce, then adds a scoop of chilled wild rice and a scoop of Mary's smoked-trout mixture of flaked smoked trout, grated cheddar cheese and diced green onions, leeks or chives in season. The salad is accompanied by a whipped horseradish crème with paprika. This combination perfectly complements the smoky, salty flavor of locally smoked trout. Garnished with tomatoes and lemon slices, the salad has a festive presentation.

At most restaurants, a signature dish would stay exactly the same, but our Smoked Trout Salad has evolved as each chef contributed a new twist. Chef Miller deconstructed the basic ingredients of the smoked-trout mix. Chef Keen initiated use of mixed micro greens drizzled with a tart lemon vinaigrette.

Our current Chef Matt Chingo's evolution involves smoking the trout and whitefish in house. Chef Chingo marinates the fillets in soy sauce, pineapple juice and a few secret ingredients. He then puts it into the smoker, with apple and hickory wood chips and charcoal.

Presentation of the Smoked Trout Salad now adds a touch of elegance, beginning with the mixed greens and chilled wild rice. The perfectly smoked fish fillet is gently placed on top, and the dish is garnished with tomatoes and diamonds of artisan aged-cheddar cheese.

I love this salad both ways. The classic works best with the smoked fish from local fisheries. The flaked trout combines nicely with the cheese and onions adding moisture, while the horseradish dressing dampens the stronger fish flavors. The contemporary recipe works best for smoked fish with a slightly sweet flavor as it lets the fish stand alone atop a nice bed of tangy, citrusy greens with a dash of cracked salt and pepper. Try both and see what you think. Then perhaps you'll create an evolution of your own.

# Smoked Lake Trout Salad (Classic)

Serves 4-6
Prep Time: 20 minutes
Cook Time: 5 minutes

**Chef's tip:** When we smoke our own fish, we smoke it for about six hours. We also smoke scallops, but the time is only about 20 minutes, just enough to give them a mild smoky flavor.

## Ingredients

1 pound smoked lake trout, boned and flaked
1 cup aged cheddar, grated
6 green onions, sliced
12 ounces mixed greens
1/2 cup Lemon Vinaigrette for greens (see recipe page 105)
pinches of salt and pepper
1 dozen grape tomatoes, sliced
1 cup cooked wild rice, chilled
lemon wedges to garnish

## Instructions

Blend the first three ingredients for the trout mixture. Toss mixed greens, salt and pepper with Lemon Vinaigrette in mixing bowl. Arrange greens on chilled plate. Top with wild rice and tomatoes, then place trout mixture (you can form it as we have here or simply use a healthy scoop). Garnish with lemons. You can also add Horseradish Cream Sauce, shown here, for dipping. See recipe on page 65.

# Smoked Lake Trout Salad
## (Contemporary)

Serves 6
Prep Time: 15 minutes
Cook Time: 5 minutes

## Ingredients

8 ounces mixed greens
1-1/2 cups cooked wild rice, chilled
1 cup or 1/2 pound smoked lake trout,
   boned and flaked
1/2 cup aged Wisconsin cheddar
   cheese, cut in small diamonds, cubes
   or crumbled
3/4 cup Lemon Vinaigrette
   (see recipe page 105)
1/2 red onion, thinly sliced
sea salt and fresh ground black pepper
   to taste
1/4 cup fresh-snipped chives, parsley
   leaves and small dill sprigs

## Instructions

In large salad bowl gently toss all ingredients except for fresh herb leaves. Season to taste with salt and a healthy grinding of black pepper, reserving a few attractive pieces of cheddar. Divide onto 6 plates and garnish with cheese and herbs.

Delicious optional garnishes might include soft poached or hard-boiled egg, sun-gold or regular cherry tomatoes in season, sliced ramps or bacon.

# Raspberry Vinaigrette

Serves 12-14
Prep time: 15 minutes
Cook Time: 5 minutes

## Ingredients

1/2 cup fresh raspberries
1/4 cup sugar
1/2 cup red wine vinegar
pinch salt
1 Tablespoon honey
1 Tablespoon lemon juice
3/4 cup canola oil
3/4 cup olive oil

## Instructions

Combine raspberries and sugar in a small saucepan and cook over medium heat for about 5 minutes, until sugar has dissolved. Transfer raspberries to blender along with all ingredients except oil. Turn blender on and pour oil in a slow and steady stream. Chill before serving.

## The Spoken Menu

The orally recited dinner menu (we call it the verbal menu) is a tradition dating to the restaurant opening in 1975. The guests arrived for the opening night, but the printed menus did not. Jerry, in a panic, asked, "Mary, what are we going to do?"

"Jerry," she said calmly, "You are going out there to tell them about the menu." Being the theatrical type, Jerry ran with the challenge and the verbal menu became a hit. It also differentiated us from other restaurants.

The spoken menu was a big part of our service for years, but it was laid aside in favor of printed menus by the manager who ran the Inn while Jerry and Mary went to Santa Barbara, where Jerry was CEO at the Professional Association of Innkeepers International.

We brought the verbal menu back when they returned and nowadays, guests can choose verbal or written menus. I recommend the more theatrical dining experience. Nothing gets the mouth watering like a well delivered description, course by course, of the whole dinner menu for the evening.

# Spinach Salad
## with Warm Bacon Vinaigrette

Serves 6
Prep Time: 20 minutes
Cook Time: 10 minutes

## Ingredients

1 pound fresh spinach, cleaned and
dried
4 hard-boiled eggs, sliced
1/2 red onion, julienne sliced
1/2 cup bleu cheese, crumbled
Warm Bacon Vinaigrette
    (see recipe below)

## Instructions

For each salad make a bed of 1/2 cup spinach on a chilled plate. Arrange sliced
egg and onion on spinach. Dress salad with Warm Bacon Vinaigrette and top with
crumbled bleu cheese.

---

**Warm Bacon Vinaigrette**
1 pound raw bacon, sliced
1/2 red onion, diced
3 Tablespoons honey
1 cup cider or red wine vinegar
1-1/2 cups canola oil
1-1/2 cups olive oil
1 teaspoon garlic, minced

Cook bacon and onion until almost crispy. Strain grease and return bacon and onion
to pan. Add honey, garlic and vinegar. Whisking constantly, add oil very slowly until
all gone. It is important that only a small amount of oil is added at a time. Be patient;
it will be well worth it! Dressing may be kept refrigerated for up to 7 days. Reheat
before serving.

# Sour Cream Potato Salad

Serves 6
Prep Time: 1 hour
Cook Time: 5 minutes to assemble

## Ingredients & Instructions

### Salad

4 cups cooked potatoes, chilled and diced (baby reds recommended, skins on)
1-1/2 cups cucumber, diced
1/2 cup radishes, thinly sliced
2 Tablespoons green onions, chopped
1/2 teaspoon salt
1/4 teaspoon white pepper, ground
1/2 teaspoon garlic, minced
1/4 pound bacon, cooked extra crispy and crumbled
3 hard-boiled egg whites, diced

Mix together potatoes, cucumbers, radishes, onion, salt, pepper, garlic and crispy bacon. Add diced egg whites to potato mixture.

---

### Sour Cream Dressing

3 hard-boiled egg yolks
1/2 cup mayonnaise
1/2 cup sour cream
1/4 cup white vinegar
sugar to taste

For the dressing, mash the yolks. Combine with mayonnaise, sour cream and vinegar. Mix thoroughly.

### To Finish

Just before serving, lightly toss the salad with the dressing and sweeten to taste with sugar.

# Seared Duck Breast Salad

Serves 4-6
Prep Time: 4 hours 15 minutes (including marinating time)
Cook Time: 15 minutes

## Ingredients

4 Muscovy duck breasts, boneless, skin-on
1 Tablespoon juniper berries
2 bay leaves, crushed
2 sprigs fresh thyme
1 teaspoon fresh garlic, minced
1/2 teaspoon pepper
2 Tablespoons olive oil
1 pound arugula
1 fennel bulb, slivered
1/2 cup goat cheese, crumbled
1 cup dried cherries
1/2 cup Raspberry Vinaigrette (see recipe page 108)

## Instructions

Trim any excess silver skin off of duck and score the skin without cutting through to
the meat. Mix oil, juniper berries, bay leaves, thyme, pepper, garlic and duck. Cover
and place in refrigerator for 4 hours to marinate. Preheat sauté pan on medium-
high heat and sear duck breast, skin side down first, for about 3 minutes. Flip duck
over and sear another 3 minutes. Set aside and let rest. Cooking the duck for this
recommended time will cook it to approximately medium-rare. Cook longer if
desired. Mix arugula, salt, pepper and raspberry vinaigrette. Slice duck breasts into
pieces. Top salad with dried cherries, cheese, fennel and duck.

# Guests, Fun and Foibles

## A Joyful Juggling Act

Multi-tasking, I submit, did not originate with the computer age. It started with the first innkeeper.

Owning and operating an inn and restaurant brings to mind all of the clichés – wearing many hats, juggling too many balls in the air, running around like a chicken with your head cut off – okay, maybe not all clichés fit, but being an innkeeper does have challenges. Whenever I hear someone say, "I'd like to retire and run a B&B," I have to laugh because the truth is, they will probably work harder than they ever imagined. Part of our job as innkeepers is to harness energy and chaos, turn it into the ultimate guest experience every time, and make it all look effortless.

As our business has grown, so have the complications. For Wendy and me, it's a lot different from when Mary and Jerry started out taking the occasional guest into their home. That was before there were 20 rooms, three buildings and the full-time restaurant.

We track deliveries and stock a bar and a full-service restaurant. We keep atop the needs for linens and maintenance supplies for three properties. We manage a staff of about 40 in the summer and have department heads who report to us. We organize a system for reservations, maintain an accounting procedure, oversee a website and marketing plan and take the occasional photo to show off a room – or better, hire a professional. We become I.T. people, keeping the Internet available and the computers running. We often check people into their rooms and seat them for dinner. On days when we don't have enough staff – as happened with the unexpected winter explosion of guests to see the ice caves in 2014 –we make beds, launder sheets and towels, and clean rooms.

We try to make every meal special and every room an unexpected pleasure for our guests. Praise from a guest is our ultimate reward, but their constructive criticism is also like gold to us. Nearly 100 percent of the time, everything runs smoothly and the staff, which becomes like a family, works in harmony. The guests, who also become like family, add to the pleasant mix.

And then there are the occasional anomalies – times when you end up with a giant sinkhole in the street, a bathtub full of gelatin, a wayward skunk headed into the basement or a letter presenting a 16-year-old complaint. Yes, some days as an innkeeper can be quite interesting …

The foyer in Le Château features quarter-sawn oak boards.

# J-E-L-L-oh, oh

"I give them three days," Jerry said as the young newlyweds struggled out of the Inn, overladen with camping gear.

"No," Mary shook her head wisely. "One day. They'll never make it."

The tale of this young couple who visited in the mid-1970s has become legend at the Rittenhouse. It's the kind of story that makes other innkeepers nod their heads in understanding, and then shake their heads in amazement. As Jerry tells it, the story unfolded like this:

They were on their honeymoon. He was in his 30s; she was in her 20s. He appeared to be the hardened, outdoors kind of guy who taught survival courses. She was the most delicate, fair-skinned flower one could imagine, not more than 105 pounds.

They spent one night at the Inn after bringing in tons of gear. They intended to take a seven-night "Adam-and-Eve" camping trip in the Apostle Islands, frolicking *au naturel* in nature. The new husband kept proudly telling Jerry he'd packed a copy of *The Joy of Sex* as a guide and they were "working their way through the book."

The next morning a water taxi was to take them to one of the islands. After an early breakfast, Eve struggled down the staircase with a gigantic 90-pound pack on her back. Jerry feared she'd take out the banister or a stained glass window, but she made it. Soon Adam bounced down after her and they both went out the door. That's when Jerry and Mary planned their little side bet – would the couple last three days or one?

A day and a half later, the couple, looking miserable, struggled back in the door. Eve was entirely covered in welts. Her hair was a mess, her face dirty and her demeanor clearly not happy. They booked the one room we had free, and Eve went upstairs to clean up. Adam described going out to the island for a secluded, romantic week with no radio or CB. They packed *The Joy of Sex*; but were unaware of the despair of black fly season, which can be bad for about a week each summer, especially on the remote islands. We asked if they had brought insect repellent. "Yes," Adam said, "but it only lasted about an hour before the flies ate through it like an appetizer."

Luckily, they had been able to flag down a fishing tug. Their camping romance nipped in the bud (by black flies), the couple decided to make good use of our nicest room and that book, as Adam again informed Jerry, page by page.

A luminous twilight at Old Rittenhouse Inn.

It was midsummer, our high season for tourism, and our Inn was full at the time. We still had only one communal hall bathroom, which Jerry cleaned between each guest in the mornings. Just as our couple finished one morning, Jerry hurried upstairs, opened the bathroom door to clean and discovered that the entire tub was filled with a brown gelatinous substance with a fruity odor. It was Jello – *The Joy* apparently recommended a bath for two in the jiggly substance. It was brown because in small-town Bayfield, the couple had to buy every flavor on the shelf to get enough. The resulting mix, we speculated, made the unappetizing bronze hue.

Jerry was absolutely panicked and other guests were in line to use the bathroom. Could he really flush the gelatin down the drain or would it destroy the septic system? Jerry turned on the hottest water and slowly melted the mess away. Not long after the brown Jello incident, we decided each room must have its own bathroom.

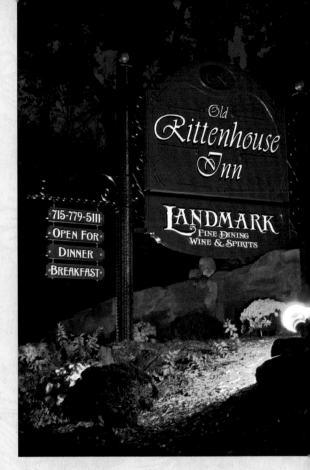

# Pépé Le P-U

Owning an Inn is not all glamour and filet mignon. Often unique problems arise, especially in an area so very close to nature.

We've had a couple run-ins, for example, with skunks. Don't get me wrong, I love all God's creatures, but there is something about the funk of a skunk that you do NOT want around your business … ever!

One summer in the mid-1980s we had an epidemic of skunks in Bayfield. Whole families with those iconic black-and-white stripes would confidently waddle down main street in the middle of the day as pedestrians scrambled to get out of the way.

One evening a local police officer was out shooting skunks to "re-educate the population," as she said (these were different times). Marlene spied a fat skunk tottering up the Inn's driveway. She aimed and expertly fired her service revolver just as the skunk made a break for our cellar. Marlene was a crack shot. The mortally wounded skunk lurched down the cellar steps and expired at the bottom. The cordite smell from the revolver hung in the air for about five seconds until an odorous plague of fresh skunk juice utterly obscured it.

Now all this would have been bad enough, but unfortunately, our kitchen fan – the large, industrial-strength one that pulled cool outside air into the kitchen – sat in a window just above the dead skunk. By the time a weeping, confused dishwasher could turn off the fan, everyone in the kitchen was covered in skunk oil. In the dining room, dinner was being served as usual until the putrid stench wafted through the kitchen door and drove both staff and guests out of the building in tears.

With no hope of continuing dinner service, we found other places for our guests to dine. Then the staff spent the rest of the night bathing every downstairs surface in tomato juice, wiping down all the walls in the kitchen and cleaning everything several times.

After working through the night, and on just one hour of sleep, we welcomed guests back the next morning for breakfast. Believe it or not, everything was back to normal.

# A Complaint 16 Years in the Making

No hospitality establishment escapes a complaint or two, though we've been exceedingly blessed by praise from our guests. When a problem does arise, we can usually make things right to the customer's satisfaction. We appreciate hearing any complaint while the guest is still here so that we can make it better immediately. Sometimes, though, a guest will wait to air a concern …

In 1992, a complaint letter arrived at the Inn. Amazingly specific in detail – though addressed "to whom it may concern" – it zeroed in on a creaking bed with an old quilt, a fireplace that smoked and a room with a chair that, as the woman wrote, "to be kind, you might call an antique, but truly it's just a piece of old furniture."

Well, we had long since replaced that bed, fixed the chimney, and retired that chair, but one thing puzzled us – this woman said she had visited in 1976, the first full year we had guests. Why wait 16 years to send the complaint?

Her friends, it turns out, were to blame – just too many of them had been raving about how phenomenal their stay was at Old Rittenhouse Inn. She simply couldn't contain her frustration any more. She didn't ask for anything, she just wanted to let off the steam that had been building, and to tell us that she doubted the credibility of her friends. Her experience at our Inn had not been so exceptional – 16 years ago.

At the time the letter came, Mary was in the hospital recovering from a stroke, and we were under immense pressure to keep things together during a busy summer at the Inn. The letter made one of our employees, who had a sharp sense of humor, so angry that she proceeded to go on a rant. The more she ranted, the funnier Jerry found the whole situation. Soon he began laughing aloud. (My dad always lives on the bright side.)

When they started their business, Jerry and Mary agreed that every letter deserved a personal response. In his reply, Jerry apologized for the room and explained that in the 16 intervening years, we certainly had made improvements. He wrote that he was sorry she'd

An inviting space in the living room at Le Château.

carried this burden so long and that her friends' praise had prompted her to write this stern letter. He invited her to come back to Bayfield and stay again, at no expense, to see for herself how we'd improved.

Finally, he sent a full refund for the 1976 price of her room, including tax: $8.50.

I don't remember if she cashed the check, but she never did use the gift certificate for the free stay.

# Return Guests

"Look at you!" Julie exclaimed when the young woman arrived with her family. "Oh my gosh – you're a beautiful grown-up woman."

It had been awhile since Julie had seen Amber Leifheit. Her parents have been coming to the Inn for more than 15 years, from the time Amber was just a little strawberry blonde girl.

Now it was a 20-year-old who greeted Julie, hugging her and saying, "We were wondering if you'd be here so we could say hello."

We have all kinds of guests at Old Rittenhouse Inn, even a few famous folk like the actor Ben Kingsley (here to scout movie locations) and the Gallo brothers (of wine-making fame). But it's our repeat guests, those who return year after year, that are one of the best perks of being an innkeeper. We're fortunate in the number of guests who return annually.

Sometimes we lose touch for a time, but then it's like homecoming when they return. For a time, the Martins came every summer. She was statuesque in her elegant dinner gowns. Ever the gentleman, he pulled out the chair for her at dinner. They sat, absorbed in each other, speaking quietly as they dined.

Then one year, they didn't return, nor did they for the next several years.

Suddenly, out of the blue one day, in walked Mr. Martin. At the reception desk, we gave a great cheer and had hugs all around. We were so tickled to see him again. Mrs. Martin, though, was not with him.

He explained that she had been very ill for a long time. Though they wanted to return, her illness prevented them from making the trip. After her passing, Mr. Martin stayed away; it would be too painful to return alone.

Now, though, he had fallen in love again. He brought her to the Inn, one of his favorite places, to create more memories. We were thrilled to be part of his life again.

Some familiar faces return now only in our memories. Year after year, Sharon and Al Brunk stayed at least a week. They loved the fresh fish and ate trout or whitefish every night. Al and Sharon were incredibly active. They were avid cross-country skiers and hikers who knew their way around all the local trails. We thought of them during the snowy winter we had in 2014, when the ice caves exploded in popularity. Al and Sharon would have loved it, and we would be sure to serve fish (and pie) for the week.

Every Christmas season, we can count on a visit from Jerry and Doreen Liljedahl. They stay in Suite X and besides their normal luggage and cold weather gear, they bring along their own Christmas tree, decorations and gifts. With no TV and the kids grown and busy, the couple can spend a quiet, joyful time here opening presents, talking and reading.

The Kaufman family first visited one summer when I was still in high school. Since that first visit, we've enjoyed their company in both summer and winter, and they often attend our Wassail Dinner Concerts during the holiday season. The Kaufmans love to spend time with their two boys in the winter wonderland of Bayfield. Now we are seeing the grandchildren, too, as the Kaufmans' son, Derek, and his wife, Leora, have a beautiful family of their own.

Barry and Arline Kaufman truly felt like family since that first year they arrived. One time, they were in the region to drop off their other son, Brett, at summer camp near Hayward. I told them my band was playing a bar gig in Hayward, and sure enough they showed up to support me. I fear they may have been horrified to find themselves in a

Guests sometimes simply like to relax on the Old Rittenhouse Inn porch with a cool beverage. Jerry and Ben Kingsley posing by the Old Rittenhouse Inn sign (nice work, Dad!)

smoky bar listening to loud rock, but they stayed for a few songs and to say "Hello." Years later, we still laugh about that night whenever we see each other.

The Kaufmans are so much like family that one year Arline hung out in the kitchen with my Aunt Julie as she cooked lasagna sauce for our own big family get-together. Arline took good notes and recently told Julie that she still makes the sauce exactly that same way, slow-cooked and seasoned with wine, herbs and garlic.

Bob and Norma Shaub rarely stayed at the Inn – they had a summer home on Madeline Island – but they always ate dinner at the Landmark. Bob, a non-drinker, always ordered a glass of Gewurtztraminer for Norma and then sipped the standard tasting pour before declaring it perfect and handing it off to Norma. It was the gentlemanly thing to do. Aunt Julie generally served their table and she kept on hand fresh brewed iced tea – Bob's preferred beverage. His other favorite was our chocolate torte, which he pronounced "the best ever." We've made sure it was on the menu whenever the Shaubs came to dinner.

It's the only natural thing to do when you've got "family" coming to visit.

# A Last Visit, A Lasting Impression

More often than you might realize, we, as innkeepers, get to celebrate special occasions in our guests' lives. More rarely, we get to do something more – to be part of a defining moment with a deeper meaning.

In the summer of 2013, a man booked Suite X as a gift for his wife. She had multiple sclerosis and used a wheelchair. We suggested a first-floor room, but only Suite X, on the third floor, met his desires for a truly special stay.

When they arrived, Lance, one of our most gifted servers, helped them get that wheelchair upstairs. In the room, as per the husband's arrangements, bouquets of flowers were placed everywhere, a plate of sweets sat on a table, and mementos of their years

Lake Superior on the horizon from the yard of Old Rittenhouse Inn.

together were lovingly placed throughout the room.

The husband asked for dinner to be served in the room, so Lance got a table with linens and set it up there. The husband had brought his own china and glasses, candles and more flowers. Lance described the night's menu aloud in mouth-watering detail. Then he carried their wonderful five-course meal, course by course, to the third floor. The wife was so elated that she was in tears.

We repeated the service for breakfast, and when it came time for check out, they said with gratitude that they didn't want to leave. Julie helped the husband get the woman in her wheelchair down the stairs. "Don't worry," Julie told her when she seemed frightened of the descent. "We've both got you."

On the first floor, the wife, overcome with emotion, had difficulty expressing how incredible we and her husband had made her feel. With her progressive disease, she knew another such visit would be unlikely, but she also knew how much love and energy her husband had put into making one weekend something that she – and all of us – will always remember.

# Sorbets

# Cranberry Stout Sorbet

Serves 10-12
Prep time: 30 minutes
Cook/Freeze Time: 2 hours 30 minutes (+ freeze time)

## Ingredients

2 cups fresh cranberries
1 bottle Guinness (12 ounces) or your favorite stout
2-1/2 cups water
2 cups sugar (adjust to taste)
3/4 cup lemon juice, fresh squeezed
1/3 cup orange juice, fresh squeezed

## Instructions

In 4-quart stock pot add cranberries, water, sugar, citrus juices and bring to boil. Boil until cranberries burst, about 15 minutes. In blender, purée cranberries in batches until they are as smooth as possible (use caution blending hot liquids). Force through sieve into bowl, discarding solids. Chill about 2 hours. Whisk in Guinness and transfer mixture to ice cream maker and freeze according to manufacturer's directions. Cover and freeze for 2 hours. For a festive touch, garnish with a sprig of mint.

# Blueberry Port Sorbet

Serves 8-10
Prep Time: 30 minutes
Cook/Freeze Time: 2 hours 30 minutes

## Ingredients

1 bottle port wine (0.75 liter), reduced by 80 percent
1 cup sugar
1-1/2 cups water
1/2 teaspoon salt
6 cups fresh blueberries
1/4 cup lemon juice, fresh squeezed

## Instructions

Simmer port wine in a pot about 20 minutes to reduce by 80 percent. Set aside to cool. In a medium saucepan, make a syrup by combining sugar, water and salt and cook over medium heat until sugar has dissolved, about 4 minutes. In a blender, purée blueberries with syrup and lemon juice. Pour through sieve and discard solids. Add port reduction and transfer sorbet mix to ice cream maker and freeze according to manufacturer's directions. Cover and freeze for 2 hours.

Berries abound in Bayfield from wonderful growers like here at Blue Vista Farm with its barn of field stone.

# Peach Moscato Sorbet

Serves 8-10
Prep Time: 2 hours 30 minutes
Cook/Freeze Time: 2 hours 30 minutes

## Ingredients

1 bottle Moscato (0.75 liter)
2/3 cup sugar
1 cup water
2-1/2 pounds ripe peaches, peeled, halved and pitted
1 teaspoon lemon zest
3 Tablespoons lemon juice, fresh squeezed

## Instructions

Pour Moscato into 4-quart stock pot and simmer to reduce by 50 percent (about 20 minutes). Add water, sugar, peaches, lemon juice and zest. Bring to boil, reduce to simmer for 15 minutes. Purée in blender and pour through sieve, discarding solids. Cool for 2 hours. Transfer mixture to ice cream maker and freeze according to manufacturer's directions. Cover and freeze for 2 hours.

# Gingered Lemon Sorbet

Serves 8-10
Prep Time: 10 minutes
Cook/Freeze Time: 2 hours 30 minutes

## Ingredients

3 cups lemon juice, fresh squeezed
3 cups orange juice, fresh squeezed
3 cups water
4 cups sugar
1/2 cup ginger root, freshly grated
1 cup unsweetened white grape juice
blueberries and fresh mint to garnish

## Instructions

In a large pot, combine all ingredients and simmer until sugar dissolves. Place sorbet mixture into ice cream machine to process and freeze according to manufacturer's instructions. Cover and freeze for 2 hours. Garnish with blueberries and a sprig of fresh mint.

Paul L. Hayden

# Meet Your Chef

## Chef Matt

When you go to a friend's house to partake in a meal, you know your host and your cook. That knowledge, I believe, makes the meal even better. So just before we serve the entrées, I thought it might be appropriate to introduce our main chef.

Matt Chingo started at Old Rittenhouse Inn's Landmark Restaurant in 2010 after working a busy season with another local restaurant. It was that time of year when restaurants here trim seasonal staff hours. We were reducing staff, too, but realized that we needed a great No. 2 to back up our executive chef. Matt came in as a sous chef and excelled from the first frittata, knocking out of the park every assignment from simple poached eggs to complex duck confit. When our former executive chef, Steven Keen, decided to move on, we didn't even need to interview for the position. The obvious replacement was already in the kitchen.

When it comes to cooking, the grill outside Le Château (facing page) or the renovated kitchen inside the Old Rittenhouse Inn (top) are Matt Chingo's two homes away from home. When it comes to fishing, Matt's happy on just about any lake or stream in our neck of the woods.

Basically, Matt has what every restaurant owner and patron desires in a chef. He always delivers beautiful plates, on time, nice and hot, filled with delicious food. Comfortable in any culinary genre – formal gourmet to down-home cooking – Matt excels particularly in one area. He is a grill master. He's also mastered our smoker, refining the way we present our smoked trout and adding smoked scallops and smoked duck breast as menu options.

Matt has done great things with the Inn's signature dishes. Our champagne chicken, delicious comfort food as made by my mother, remains comforting and delicious in Matt's kitchen, but he's turned it into a work of art with his presentation and choice of accompaniments. The chicken is served on a bed of marscapone whipped Yukon Gold potatoes with julienne-sliced prosciutto and a drizzle of truffle oil.

I most appreciate the results of Matt's love for bourbon and bacon – two ingredients that frequently show up in his recipes. They are employed in unique ways, like using bacon to encrust shrimp or adding bourbon to enhance his barbecues.

Our chef may have been a cooking prodigy. "My grandma first started to teach me how to cook when I was 6 years old," Matt recalls. "I made a fried egg. After that I watched my mom and my grandma cooking, I wanted to know what and how they were cooking."

Matt's main approach to food is creative experimentation and his testers are often his girls, Lillian, 6, and Lucille, 2, and their mom, Megan. He admits his experiments might go awry, but often they are hits. So while the bacon-bourbon buttermilk biscuits were a bust – "They could have gone without the bourbon. I don't know what I was thinking there." – the breakfast lasagna layering pancakes, eggs, bacon and chorizo with maple béchamel sauce was a hit – "We sold the whole pan."

A perfect fit for the Rittenhouse, Matt is willing and eager to adapt to the day's bounty and pleased that our verbal specials allow flexibility.

Matt related an example of how the Landmark lets his creativity flow: Thinking about one evening's menu on his half-hour commute, Matt envisioned savory south-of-the-border fare only to discover that Jerry had bought 10 flats of raspberries. With just a slight mental turn of the road, Matt served up raspberry ancho-chile empanadas.

Most of his life, cooking and painting have been Matt's artistic outlets. He dabbled with one college semester of meteorology, but, says Matt, "I was cooking at this steak and seafood restaurant in North Carolina with a very knowledgeable chef who pointed me in the right direction. I didn't have time for school; I was making good money and I asked myself why do something I'm unsure I'll like when I know I love to cook."

Born in Ashland, Wisconsin, Matt finds this region suits him. When not in the kitchen, Matt is outdoors fishing, hunting or snowshoeing. He often shows me pictures of the fish he's caught. I'm a fisherman, too, but I don't seem to have the luck Matt has at bringing in the big ones. Most skilled fisherman think like a fish, so I hear, and based on his stringer, Matt definitely knows what's on a trout's mind.

Although he has no formal culinary training, when Matt's thinking like a chef, few can match his natural talent. We're pleased that he's chosen to continue his career here, and his art can be found throughout this cookbook.

# Entrées

# Champagne Chicken
# (Poulet aux Champignons)

Serves 4-6
Prep Time: 2 hours 30 minutes
Cook Time: 40 minutes

## Ingredients

4 chicken breasts, boneless, skin-off
1 teaspoon fresh garlic, minced
1/4 teaspoon pepper
1/2 teaspoon fresh thyme leaves
4 Tablespoons olive oil, divided
8 ounces prosciutto, julienned
4 ounces Roasted Mushrooms (see recipe page 156), reserve some for garnish
1 batch Champagne Grand Marnier Sauce (see recipe page 168)

## Instructions

Combine first 5 ingredients in a large bowl except for 2 tablespoons oil. Place chicken in refrigerator to marinate for 2 hours. Preheat 2 sauté pans with oil on medium heat. In one pan, sear chicken breasts for about 6 minutes on each side or until done. Combine the mushrooms and Champagne Grand Marnier Sauce in the other pan and heat. Plate chicken and pour sauce over it, garnish with mushrooms and prosciutto. Serve with your favorite starch! (We like Marscapone Whipped Yukon Gold Potatoes, see recipe page 154.)

# Seared Duck
## with Wild Plum Maple Glaze

Serves 4
Prep Time: 30 minutes
Cook Time: 15 minutes

## Ingredients

4 duck breasts, 6 to 8 ounces each, skin-on
24 wild plums or black plums, pitted and cut in halves
3/4 to 1 cup maple syrup, depending on tartness of plums
2 cups unsalted chicken stock
1-1/2 teaspoons fresh lemon juice
salt and pepper to taste

## Instructions

Score the duck skins and season with salt and pepper, then sear over medium heat to desired doneness. Remove to a warm place to rest. Add plums to the pan and sear on high heat for 30 seconds. Add chicken stock, maple syrup, lemon juice, salt and pepper. Reduce heat and cook until thick. Pour mixture over duck breasts and serve. Pan-seared polenta and wilted spinach or wild rice make wonderful side dishes.

# Duck Confit in Spinach Crêpes
## with Wild Blueberry Gastrique

Not for beginners! This is a recipe with a higher degree of difficulty and it takes time, but it is well worth the effort. The technique is derived from an ancient method of preserving meat by salting the pork, duck or chicken and slowly cooking it in its own fat. It's packed tightly and covered in the cooking fat, which seals and preserves the meat and concentrates flavor. In modern times it is acceptable to cheat by using pre-rendered duck fat, which is a glorious thing!

Serves 4
Prep Time: 24 hours 30 minutes (includes marinating time)
Cook Time: 4 hours

## Ingredients & Instructions

### Duck Confit
2 Muscovy duck legs with thighs attached
   (also works great with free range chicken)
2 Tablespoons olive oil
3 bay leaves, crushed
1 Tablespoon juniper berries
1 teaspoon fresh thyme
1 teaspoon black pepper
2 cups duck fat

Place the above ingredients, except the duck fat, together and seal in an airtight container. Marinate in refrigerator for 24 hours. Preheat oven to 200° F. Take duck parts out of container, rinse off and pat dry. Place skin side down in glass pan and cover with 2 cups warm duck fat. Place into oven and cook for about 4 hours. When fork tender, remove from fat and let cool. Pull meat off bones into bite-sized pieces and set aside for immediate use.

---

### Spinach Crêpes
 1 cup all-purpose flour
 2 eggs
1/2 cup milk
1/2 cup water
1/4 teaspoon salt
2 Tablespoons butter, melted
1 cup fresh spinach

Place all the ingredients in blender except spinach. After everything is thoroughly

blended, add spinach and blend until smooth. Heat a lightly oiled griddle or frying pan over medium high heat. Pour or scoop the batter onto the griddle, using approximately 1/4 cup for each crêpe. Tilt the pan with a circular motion so that the batter coats the surface evenly. Cook the crêpe for about 2 minutes, until the bottom is light brown. Loosen with a spatula, turn and cook the other side.

## Confit Filling for Crêpes

Duck Confit as per recipe
1 Tablespoon lemon zest
1 Tablespoon fresh lemon juice
1 cup mascarpone
1 cup cooked wild rice
salt and pepper to taste
1 teaspoon fresh tarragon, chopped
1 teaspoon fresh thyme, chopped
1 teaspoon fresh parsley, chopped

Preheat oven to 350° F. Combine all the above ingredients and mix thoroughly. Place about 1/2 cup of filling in each crêpe at the 7 o'clock position. Fold in half, then into quarters. Place on pan and bake enough to rewarm everything (10 to 15 minutes).

## Gastrique

1 cup granulated sugar
3 Tablespoons water
1 cup apple cider vinegar
2 cups wild blueberries

Measure out the vinegar and keep it handy. Place the sugar and water in a heavy-bottom pan and set over medium-high heat. Stir just enough to wet the sugar (it should look like wet sand) then leave it alone to melt and start to caramelize. When the liquid sugar starts to turn color at the edges slowly swirl the pan to evenly distribute the browning sugar. Cook the sugar to a dark amber and pull it from the heat just as it starts to smoke. Moving quickly, tilt the pan away from you and pour in the vinegar. It will splatter, so be careful! When it all settles, place it back over medium heat and scrape any hardened sugar from the bottom of the pan, stirring it to reincorporate it into the vinegar. Add the berries and continue to cook over medium heat until the gastrique is reduced slightly and achieves a syrupy consistency, 5-10 minutes. Remove from the heat, cover and keep warm.

## To finish

Plate the crêpes and drizzle with the warm gastrique.

# Steak Bercy
## with Bercy Sauce

Serves 4-6
Prep Time: 45 minutes
Cook Time: 30 minutes

# Ingredients

4 filet mignon (4-8 ounces each)
1 batch Bercy Sauce (see recipe below)
1 cup Roasted Mushrooms (see recipe page 156)

# Instructions

Preheat charcoal or gas grill. Season steaks with salt and pepper and grill to your liking. Add mushrooms to Bercy sauce and serve with steaks.

---

**Bercy Sauce**
2 cups dry red wine
2 shallots, rough chopped
2 sprigs thyme
12 peppercorns
2 bay leaves
1 cup veal demi-glace
1 teaspoon fresh garlic, minced
salt and pepper to taste

> **Chef's tip:** This Bercy Sauce is great with broiled or grilled meat or fish, as well as with our Steak Bercy. There are actually two sauces named after the Bercy section of Paris. The "other Bercy" is a sauce for fish, and is essentially a reduction of white wine, fish stock, shallots, and seasonings.

Combine all ingredients in a 2-quart sauce pot except demi-glace and garlic. Cook over medium heat and reduce by 80 percent. Put demi-glace into a different pot and pour reduction through sieve into it. Add garlic and simmer for 10 minutes. Salt and pepper to taste.

# Lamb & Pine Nut Meatballs
## with Pumpkin Gnocchi, Black Olives & Sage

Serves 6
Prep Time: 2 hours 30 minutes
Cook Time: 30 minutes

## Ingredients & Instructions

### Meatballs
3-1/2 pounds lean ground lamb
2 cups pine nuts, divided
1 shallot, rough chopped
1 garlic clove
2 Tablespoons red wine vinegar
2 eggs
1/2 cup packed Italian parsley leaves and chives, minced
1/2 fennel bulb, core removed
2 Tablespoons extra virgin olive oil
1 Tablespoon kosher salt
1/4 teaspoon black pepper, freshly ground
pinch each ground cinnamon, ground clove and chili powder

In bowl of food processor put 1-1/3 cups of the pine nuts and begin to purée. With processor still running, add shallot, garlic and vinegar. Add eggs and continue to purée until very smooth. Add herbs and fennel and purée until finely chopped. Add olive oil and pulse until emulsified. In large bowl mix ground lamb with pine-nut mixture, remainder of pine nuts, kosher salt, pepper and other spices just until mixed. Form into 2-inch balls and chill thoroughly. Makes about 25.

--------

### Gnocchi
1 cup puréed roast pumpkin. We like Cinderella pumpkins for their great flavor, but any will do, including winter squash such as kuri or butternut.
1 egg
1/2 cup high-gluten flour (may need more)
pinch salt

Put on a large pot of salted water to boil. Mix pumpkin purée with egg and add salt. Fold in the flour little by little until the dough comes together. It should have the consistency of thick mashed potatoes. On a floured board, roll the dough into 1/2-inch thick cylinders and cut pieces 1-inch long (this may take much more flour). A piping bag with a round tip works well, too.

If you use the piping bag, simply squeeze over the rapidly boiling water while cutting 1-inch pieces with a paring knife. Otherwise drop your rolled gnocchi in the water a handful at a time, taking care they do not stick together. When the dumplings float, they are ready and should be pulled out with a small strainer or perforated ladle and spread out on a lightly greased tray. We typically give them a light coating of pan spray at this point to prevent sticking. Place the tray in the refrigerator or freezer to chill. The gnocchi may be kept a couple days in the fridge or a few weeks in the freezer. We prefer to keep them frozen right up until it's time to cook them.

## To finish

about 30 black or Kalamata olives, pitted
   and halved
30 whole leaves fresh sage
3 cups good chicken or vegetable stock
2-4 Tablespoons unsalted butter (optional)
salt and fresh ground pepper to taste
toasted pumpkin seeds to garnish
cooking oil for pans

Heat large skillet or roasting pan. Add cooking oil and sear meatballs on all sides. Take care that the sides touching the pan are fully brown before moving the meatballs or they may stick. Cook to desired doneness; they are great anywhere from medium to well done. Takes 5-10 minutes.

Heat a frying pan with small amount of cooking oil. Over medium-high heat, fry the gnocchi, straight from fridge or freezer, tossing occasionally, until they become golden brown. Add sage leaves and allow to fry a bit. Toss in olives and stock, boil 2 minutes, season to taste with salt and pepper. Swirl in butter to melt. Serve up a pile of gnocchi in the center of the plate. Add the sauce from the pan, meatballs and garnish with the toasted pumpkin seeds or "pepitas."

# Apple-Glazed Pork Porterhouse

Serves 4-6
Prep Time: 40 minutes
Cook Time: 2 hours 30 minutes

## Ingredients & Instructions

### Pork Porterhouse

4 pork porterhouse chops (about 1 pound each)
1 Tablespoon pepper
1/2 Tablespoon salt
2 teaspoons granulated garlic
2 teaspoons onion powder
2 teaspoons Montreal steak seasoning (this Canadian steak spice is carried by several brands)

Season pork with above ingredients. Preheat 2 large sauté pans over medium-high heat and sear pork on each side for about 5 minutes. Set aside.

### Stock

1/2 bottle red wine (0.75 liter)
4 cups water
1 onion, diced
2 Tablespoons ham base
1 Tablespoon chicken base
1 Tablespoon beef base
3 bay leaves
1 Tablespoon coriander
4 cloves garlic, halved
3 sprigs tarragon
3 sprigs thyme
3 sprigs basil
3 sprigs rosemary
12 peppercorns

### Roux

2 Tablespoons butter, melted
4 Tablespoons all-purpose flour
2 cups stock from saucepan after chops are done

Preheat oven to 350° F. Combine stock ingredients in a large saucepan and bring to a boil. Reduce to a simmer and cook for 15 minutes. Pour stock into roasting pan and add seared pork. Cover with foil and braise in oven for 2-1/2 hours. After pork is done, remove 2 cups of stock and place in saucepan for gravy, thickening with the roux. Plate and top pork with your favorite apple cider marmalade (ours, of course, can be purchased from Rittenhouseinn.com). Pour gravy on and around chop to finish.

# En Croute de la Mer
## with a Curried Beurre Blanc Sauce

Serves 4-6
Prep Time: 40 minutes
Cook Time: 2 hours 30 minutes

## Ingredients

8 ounces filo dough
1 pound trout, skinned and boned (or salmon)
1 pound whitefish, skinned and boned
salt and pepper to taste
fresh herbs of choice, such as dill and tarragon
1 cup fresh spinach
1/2 cup olive oil

## Instructions

Preheat oven to 400° F. Layer 8-10 filo dough sheets on top of one another, brushing each with olive oil. Using a third of the spinach, make a layer down the center of the filo stack. Place trout fillet on top of the spinach and season with salt and pepper. Distribute another third of the spinach, layering it on top of the trout. Generously sprinkle on the fresh herbs. Place the whitefish fillet on the second spinach layer and season with salt and pepper. Use the remaining spinach as a final layer to cover the whitefish. Fold the edges of the filo toward the middle, wrapping them around the fish/spinach. On a baking dish, place the "envelope" seam side down. Bake for 25-30 minutes until crisp and brown. Slice and serve with Beurre Blanc.

---

**Curried Beurre Blanc**
2 cups white wine
6 cloves garlic, minced
1 shallot, minced
2-4 stems thyme and tarragon
1 teaspoon curry powder
10 peppercorns
10 whole coriander seeds
salt to taste
1/4 cup heavy cream
1-1/2 cups unsalted butter, cubed

> **Chef's tip:** If the butter is added while the sauce is too hot, the sauce will break.

Except for the butter, boil all ingredients until reduced to about 2/3 of a cup. Take the sauce off the heat and let it cool 3-4 minutes before adding the butter. Whisk until the butter is fully incorporated. Strain sauce through a fine strainer and serve as a sauce for the En Croute.

# Reddened Lake Trout or Whitefish

Serves 8
Prep time: 5 minutes
Cook Time:15 minutes

## Ingredients

4 pounds fresh lake trout or
   whitefish fillets (8 fillets)
1 cup bread crumbs
1/2 cup dry dill, chopped
3 Tablespoons garlic powder
1 Tablespoon salt
1/2 cup Rittenhouse Reddening
   (see recipe next page)
1/2 cup melted butter

## Instructions

Process bread crumbs, dill, garlic powder, salt and reddening in a food processor with a steel blade. Cover flesh side of fillet with crumb mixture.

Add melted butter to a large skillet and place fillet skin down. Cover and cook until fish flakes. Remove fish from sauté pan and remove skin. Serve on warm plates, with the sauce (see recipe next page) to garnish.

# Fresh from the Lake

How do you like your fish? At Landmark Restaurant, "fresh" is the first answer, an easy one with Lake Superior nearby and commercial fishermen bringing a daily bounty of fresh lake trout or whitefish in season.

Beyond that, there are many wonderful ways to prepare fish or to create the best food pairing combinations. In this cookbook, you'll find a few of our favorite options.

One great seasoning for our freshwater fish is reddening, a milder version of the blackening spice famous in Cajun cooking. It adds warmth rather than heat, and imparts a delicious flavor. Wonderful for fish, it works quite nicely with chicken, too. At the Landmark, we dust the trout or whitefish fillets with the seasoning, and then pan-sear, bake or broil them. Mary contributed this very versatile "reddening" seasoning many years ago and we still enjoy it today.

We mainly use these two types of fish, although herring (cisco) is popular on some Lake Superior shores. For those less familiar with our freshwater fish, trout tends to be more oily and may have a more definite "fish" taste than the milder whitefish. Both are excellent.

## Reddening Sauce

1 cup butter, softened
1 Tablespoon fresh garlic, minced
2 Tablespoons Rittenhouse Reddening
1/2 cup tomato paste
1/2 teaspoon Tabasco sauce

In a food processor fitted with a steel blade, process softened butter, fresh garlic, reddening, tomato paste, and Tabasco sauce. Warm in saucepan over low heat.

## Rittenhouse Reddening

1 part curry, ground
1 part white pepper
1 part red cayenne pepper
2 parts onion powder
3 parts garlic powder
6 parts paprika

**Chef's note:** This recipe is given in parts so you can make as much or as little as you need.

Blend all ingredients until evenly mixed throughout.

The real fish dish debate locally is not about what kind is your favorite fish, it's about skin-on or skin-off in preparation. Believe me, there are strong and differing opinions on this subject.

I prefer skin-off, but one of our former executive chefs, Dave Miller, was an absolute master at cooking trout and whitefish with the skins on. Chef Miller graduated as valedictorian of his class at the Culinary Institute of America in Hyde Park, New York. He then went on to work at L'Étoile in Madison before coming to Old Rittenhouse Inn. He has since gone on to be the chef instructor at the Culinary Institute of Virginia.

Chef Miller's skin-on trout was seasoned and seared so perfectly that the skin became crispy and delicious and the flavor was truly wonderful. Even a skin-off guy like me enjoyed it.

These days, though, you usually see all of our local fish fillets prepared sans skin, making them appealingly adaptable for different cooking techniques, sauces and seasonings.

Skins-off need not mean "naked," of course. A good fresh lemon vinaigrette with a nice micro green salad alongside … or maybe a spicier sauce made with the reddening seasoning and a squeeze of fresh lemon added for that appealing lemony scent.

One of our favorite accompaniments for fish is couscous. Many times we'll prepare it Mediterranean-style, with large-pearl Israeli couscous, basil pesto, sun-dried tomatoes and Kalamata olives (see recipe next page). It's a yummy combination.

# Lake Trout or Whitefish Piccata
## with Mediterranean Couscous & Lemon Caper Compound Butter

Serves: 4-6
Prep Time: 2 hours 30 minutes
Cook Time: 30 minutes

## Ingredients & Instructions

**Lemon Caper Compound Butter**
1 cup unsalted butter
zest of 1 lemon
1 teaspoon salt
2 Tablespoons capers

> **Chef's tip:** Lemon Caper Compound Butter pairs well with many kinds of seafood.

Combine butter, lemon zest and salt in food processor until smooth. Add capers and pulse a few times to incorporate them into the butter. Spoon onto a 12-inch sheet of plastic wrap, forming a log shape with butter. Roll plastic wrap around butter and refrigerate for 1 hour.

---

## Mediterranean Couscous
1 cup Israeli couscous (also called pearl couscous)
1/4 cup sun-dried tomato, julienned
1/4 cup Kalamata olives, halved and pitted
2 Tablespoons fresh basil, chopped
2 Tablespoons olive oil
1 teaspoon fresh garlic, minced
salt and pepper to taste

Boil the couscous to al dente as you would any other pasta. Drain and place in sauté pan with all other ingredients. Heat on low-medium for about 10 minutes.

---

## Fish
1-1/2 pounds lake trout or whitefish (4-6 ounce fillets) boned and skinned
   We recommend fresh Lake Superior fish, of course!
1 cup all-purpose flour
1 Tablespoon kosher salt
1 teaspoon white pepper
1/4 cup extra virgin olive oil

Combine flour, salt and pepper and dredge fish. Add oil to sauté pan and heat at medium heat. Once oil is preheated, sear fish on each side for 2-3 minutes.

## To finish
Place couscous on plate and top with seared fish. Remove plastic wrap from Lemon Caper Compound Butter and slice butter to desired thickness. Place butter on top of warmed fish. Enjoy!

# Interludes

## Tragedy & Helping Hands

Old Rittenhouse Inn staff and guests feel like an extended family, and the matriarch of that family is my mom, Mary Phillips. Without her, this Inn would not have been possible. It was always Mary's "other baby," her creation, her heart's dream. As a husband-wife team, Jerry and Mary worked hand in hand on many projects to make the Inn better, but Mary was our solid rock. Tough, brilliant, and nearly inexhaustible, she worked like a team of horses, and did the work of many.

This fact became most apparent after Mary's stroke in 1992. We hired eight people to fill all of her Inn jobs, yet it was still a struggle. There's no way to minimize Mary's importance to the Inn; it's impossible to downplay the many roles she played on a daily basis.

Armed with a tall Eckels Pottery mug full of strong black coffee, Mary ran the Inn from the customary perch of her kitchen stool. She cooked every meal, answered the phones, gave a pat on the head, redirected a problem or met with a supplier as needed. With the telephone in one hand and a hot sauté pan in the other, Mary conducted real estate transactions that helped save Bayfield landmarks. Her daily routine of restaurant life went hand in hand with profound moments. For Mary, it was all in a day's work.

When I heard about my mom's cerebral hemorrhage, I went into shock. I didn't know what to do. A college junior at the University of Wisconsin-Madison, I was out having fun with my roommates that February night and had just returned home when the phone rang. It was Dad. When I heard his voice, I immediately knew something was terribly wrong. Mom had had a severe stroke, he told me. I needed to get to Duluth as quickly as possible, whatever it took. He said he loved me and didn't need to say anything else.

My roommate Matt Kurtz volunteered to drive, but I didn't have a car and neither did my roommates. Not knowing what to do, I called my girlfriend, Nora, who lived across town. Of course we could use her car, she said, and within 10 minutes she arrived and helped me put a travel bag together. Everything was a blur.

Team Rittenhouse does change over time, but we don't forget our crews. Here's an early one, from left: Pat LaGrew, Lance Birkholz, Rick Thompson, Larry Bettenhauser, Mark Phillips, Paul Miller, Kris Knetter, Lois Albrecht, Jenny Albrecht, Cindy Hepner, Renée Appel, Charlene Lounsbury, Mary Hudak, Anne Carlson and Sue Beauregard. Jerry and Mary Phillips pose proudly up front.

Matt and I jumped into the car at 3 a.m. and headed for Duluth, Minnesota, some 330 miles away. Matt drove fast through the black night on roads completely unfamiliar to him. The closer we got, the worse the roads were. Filled with emotions and fear, I don't remember much about the trip, but when we finally arrived in Duluth six hours later, I got the best possible news: Mom had made it through the night, which nobody expected.

As it turns out, it was a miracle she made it to the hospital in the first place. Mom had a history of high blood pressure. Her stroke occurred suddenly, as she and Dad were relaxing in one of the empty guestrooms. Dad was at her side from that moment on. The first ambulance took her over icy roads to the Memorial Medical Center in Ashland, normally 30 minutes away. But with blowing snow, glare ice and an ambulance transfer, the trip took nearly 2 hours. The staff in Ashland quickly discerned she needed more intensive care and transferred her to a Duluth hospital.

Normally an airlift would have been the next step, but the massive mid-February blizzard created white-out conditions. The helicopter couldn't get off the ground, so an ambulance with a brave crew took her from Ashland to Duluth on the hazardous roads. It was a harrowing, agonizing ride. The ambulance could only travel 25 mph. Jerry sat in the back with Mary, holding her hand and telling her she'd be okay, to stay with him and how much he loved her.

By the time they reached Duluth, her situation was grim, but a brilliant surgeon worked through the night to save her. She was in intensive care when I arrived. Jerry asked Mary for some kind of sign that she knew we were there; she squeezed his finger with her good hand. We'll never forget that small signal.

I spent the next week at the hospital. Jerry was often there, too, but also traveled back to the Rittenhouse, trying to figure out a new plan to move forward.

Mom's initial recovery took place over the next three months at an extended-care facility near the hospital. I returned to UW-Madison. I wanted to quit for the semester, but Dad insisted I go back to finish. In hindsight, he was right. I might never have gone back otherwise.

Jerry drove to Duluth during any free time to visit Mary and boost her spirits. He was exhausted, running himself ragged, but seemed always in great spirits himself, completely optimistic. That is Jerry Phillips, my dad. He lives in the light. It's one of the traits I admire most about him.

Coming home to Bayfield for summer break was strange that year, unlike any previous summer. The surroundings were the same, but everything had changed. I lived with my parents at the Goldman house, across the ravine from the Rittenhouse. I took

Mom to physical and speech therapies and shared her great frustrations. Always a great communicator, she was limited by aphasia to "yes," "no" and a few rudimentary gestures. She knew the words in her head, but when she spoke, they came out wrong. We all had a hard time transitioning to the new reality.

Meanwhile, we headed straight into our busiest summer ever at the Inn. Jerry, our incredible staff and all the friends and supporters who loved us and believed in the Rittenhouse pulled us through that hard time. Together, they finished the cookbook Mary was working on before her stroke, *Favorite Recipes from the Old Rittenhouse Inn* (now long out of print, a few recipes are in this cookbook, such as Orange Blossom Torte and En Croute de la Mer).

With help from key staff members, Jerry led the restaurant through that first season without Mary. He took over the kitchen until we found an executive chef (which took almost a year). To Jerry's credit, most guests remained unaware that anything had changed.

Team Rittenhouse rallied. We pulled together to make it work, but 1992 was the line of demarcation: Before and After Mary's Stroke. Thankfully, our business had an amazing momentum and trajectory that allowed us to grow and prosper during those difficult years.

More than 20 years later, Mary still finds ways to be involved with the Inn, mostly through her ideas about dining and décor. She loves the Inn and Bayfield. It makes her happy to be here. She often has dinner at the restaurant, and if she has a suggestion, she certainly lets us know!

Wendy and I discuss our ideas, plans and dreams about the Inn together as a big family around the dinner table. Our kids even pipe up with ideas sometimes. For us, this works great. I have seen instances where multigenerational businesses struggle because the family fights or disagrees about how to do things. Fortunately, that has never been the case with us. Of course, like any family, we have differing opinions, but it never causes a rift or something we can't overcome.

Recently we were interviewed by a television production company looking to cast a reality TV show about an innkeeping family. During our Skype interview, they kept asking us questions like, "What things create conflict at the Inn?" and "What do you fight about?" and "How does working with your family annoy you?"

Finally, we just laughed, and I said, "Sorry, but I don't think we're right for you. We don't have the kind of drama you're looking for."

Even now that Wendy and I are responsible for operation of the Inn, we still regularly discuss our plans with Jerry and Mary. We bounce ideas off them because they have seen it all and they offer good advice. Of course, any hotel or restaurant has some natural drama and there are always personalities involved, but our family really loves each other and enjoys working together. It might not make for the best reality TV show, but it makes for a pretty great life.

# An Idea Gone South

In winter, when the guests were gone and the work done, our family piled into our Ford van and drove, usually southeasterly and often toward Savannah, Georgia, for a month-long road trip.

Like my folks, I loved Savannah. To me it was a journey into a different culture. My parents were also doing research, absorbing that southern hospitality with its unspoken, easy charm. They sampled great restaurants and wonderful hotels. (We ended up in a few terrible hotels, too, and you can learn from bad experiences, especially if you can have a good laugh about it later.)

The big city of Atlanta fascinated me, too. One night at our hotel there, a horrible altercation erupted down the hall. An awful domestic disturbance, it might have ended in a stabbing. There were sirens and too much noise to sleep at all that night, quite harrowing for a boy used to the absolute silence of a Bayfield winter night. The loudest thing we'd hear any night at home might be a foghorn, and as one of my favorite sounds, the foghorn can still lull me to sleep almost instantly. The sound evokes memories of our first years at the Inn, living on the third floor together and waking up in the wee morning hours to hear that foghorn and to know the fishermen were out in the bay.

When I was in junior high school, Mom and Dad considered selling the Old Rittenhouse Inn and moving to the East Coast, perhaps Virginia or North Carolina. We went on a few scouting trips, just driving through the countryside, looking for "For Sale" signs. In North Carolina, one mansion up for sale once belonged to the family who founded Cannon Mills and made the well-known Cannon towels.

Without an appointment and on a whim, Mom and Dad knocked on the door of the mansion, which had its "For Sale" sign outside. A kind woman welcomed them at the door. The epitome of Southern charm and hospitality, she invited them in, gave them a grand tour of the home, talked about the history of the property and the area and served them tea and sweet cakes in the parlor. It was quite magical. As they prepared to leave, Jerry took the opportunity to say, "May I inquire what your asking price is for the house? We'd love to possibly purchase it and start a wonderful country inn."

With smiling charm, she gently ushered them to the door. "Well now, of course, it has been lovely passing the time with you," she drawled sweetly, "but I would never sell my house to no damn Yankee!"

Compared to Southern charm, Bayfield charm is perhaps more agreeable. I, for one, am so happy that we stayed at the Rittenhouse, where we belonged.

# Accompaniments

# Jerry's Cranberries

Serves 6
Prep Time: 7 minutes
Cook Time: 20 minutes

> **Chef's tip:** Any frozen citrus concentrate can be used. Try orange or lemonade to see what best suits your tastes.

## Ingredients

1 bag (12 ounces) fresh or frozen cranberries
1 container (12 ounces) frozen limeade concentrate (reserve out some and blend to taste)
3/4 cup honey
1 Tablespoon orange peel, grated
1 Tablespoon ginger, grated

## Instructions

Combine cranberries, limeade concentrate and honey in a small or medium saucepan. Cook over medium heat until cranberries pop (about 15 minutes). Remove from heat. Taste to check for sweetness. If needed, add more honey to taste. Add fresh orange peel and ginger. Stir well and chill. Serve chilled as a side with your favorite holiday meal.

# Wild Rice Pilaf

Serves 6-8
Prep Time: 15 minutes
Cook Time: 1 hour

## Ingredients

2 cups uncooked wild rice
6 cups vegetable stock
1 yellow onion, diced
2 carrots, diced
1 Tablespoon granulated ancho chile
1/2 cup unsalted butter
2 bay leaves
1 teaspoon salt
1/2 teaspoon pepper

## Instructions

Place all ingredients in a pot and bring to boil. Reduce heat and place a lid on top.
Cook until rice has absorbed all of the stock, about 1 hour. (Remove bay leaves before
serving.)

# Mascarpone Whipped Yukon Golds

Serves 4-6
Prep Time: 10 minutes
Cook Time: 40 minutes

## Ingredients

1 pound Yukon Gold potatoes, peeled
1/2 cup unsalted butter
1/2 cup heavy cream
1/2 cup mascarpone cheese
1/4 teaspoon white pepper
1 teaspoon salt

**Chef's tip:** Run peeled potatoes through a food mill to make lump-free potatoes. If a food mill is not accessible, whip the potatoes as soon as you get them peeled and while they are still hot. The colder they get, the lumpier they will be.

## Instructions

Cut potatoes in half and place in pot with salted water. Boil potatoes until fork tender. Strain potatoes and let them sit for a few minutes. Place butter and cream in pot to warm up. Meanwhile, peel the skin off with your fingers and place potatoes in mixing bowl. Mix in all the remaining ingredients just until no lumps remain. Serve immediately.

# Baked Pasta
## with Brie Mornay Sauce

Serves 12
Prep Time: 25 minutes
Cook Time: 20 minutes

# Ingredients

2-1/2 pounds pasta, (cavatappi, bowtie or penne) cooked al dente
Brie Mornay Sauce (see recipe below)
3 pounds Roasted Mushrooms (see recipe page 156)
2 large onions, caramelized (see recipe page 156)
2 pounds asparagus (side dish)

# Instructions

Cook pasta in salted water. Prepare Brie Cheese Mornay Sauce, roasted mushrooms and caramelized onions. If vegetables are done ahead of time, refrigerate for future use, otherwise set aside to incorporate with the pasta and mornay sauce. This makes a nice side dish with duck.

---

**Brie Mornay Sauce**
**Roux**
½ cup unsalted butter
1 cup all-purpose flour

Melt butter on medium high heat and add flour, stirring constantly. Cook for 5 minutes to cook out the raw flour taste.

**Sauce Base**
8 cups 2% milk, boiling
2 sprigs fresh thyme
2 bay leaves
2 teaspoons garlic, minced
1 cup dry white wine
2 cups Brie cheese, rind removed
4 Tablespoons unsalted butter

In a heavy saucepan, mix all the ingredients except the Brie and butter. Bring to a boil. Add the roux, whisking constantly until all of it is incorporated into the sauce. Reduce heat and simmer for 1 hour, stirring occasionally. Whisk in the Brie and butter until completely incorporated. Strain the sauce for use and pour over pasta and vegetables.

# Roasted Mushrooms

Both recipes found on this page, the roasted mushrooms and caramelized onions, are simple to prepare yet are amazingly versatile and add so much to the dishes they enhance.

Serves 4-6
Prep Time: 10 minutes
Cook Time: 10 minutes

## Ingredients

3 pounds mushrooms, use
    something exotic. We recommend
    a blend of oyster (shown here),
    crimini, portabella and shiitake
1/3 cup olive oil, extra virgin
salt and pepper to taste

## Instructions

Preheat oven to 350° F. Spread washed, blotted-dry mushrooms on a baking sheet. Roast for 7-10 minutes. Sprinkle with oil, salt and pepper. Cool for future use.

# Caramelized Onions

Serves 4-6
Prep Time: 10 minutes
Cook Time: 20 minutes

## Ingredients

2 large onions, use your favorite kind
2 Tablespoons butter
salt and pepper to taste
1 Tablespoon sugar

## Instructions

Cook all ingredients on medium-high heat in a large skillet for 15-20 minutes, or until desired doneness. Cool for future use.

# Parsnips with Maple Syrup Glaze

Serves 6
Prep Time: 20-25 minutes
Cook Time: 20-25 minutes

## Ingredients

6 parsnips, peeled and cut into 2-3 inch strips
2 Tablespoons butter
1/4 cup water
1/4 cup maple syrup
1/3 teaspoon nutmeg, freshly grated
salt and pepper to taste

> **Chef's tip:** For color and variety, I often use 3 parsnips and 3 carrots. You can also use a sprinkle of fresh diced herbs as an aromatic garnish.

## Instructions

In a large skillet melt the butter, then add the parsnips and the water. Cover and cook on low to medium heat until water is absorbed and parsnips are soft, 12-15 minutes. Add maple syrup, sprinkle with salt and pepper and grated fresh nutmeg. Brown on medium heat until parsnips are caramelized and beautifully browned and serve.

# Apple-Rhubarb Chutney

Yields 1-1/2 quarts
Prep/Cook Time: 1 hour 30 minutes

## Ingredients

2 cups rhubarb, chopped
2 cups apples, chopped and unpeeled (we prefer Cortlands)
2 teaspoons garlic, minced
1 cup golden raisins
1 cup dark raisins
1 cup light brown sugar, firmly packed
1/2 cup honey
1/3 cup lemon peel, grated
1/3 cup orange peel, grated
2 Tablespoons orange juice concentrate
1/4 cup lemonade concentrate
1/3 cup cranberry juice concentrate
1 Tablespoon ginger root, freshly grated
3/4 teaspoon ground cinnamon
1/8 teaspoon ground cloves
1/8 teaspoon ground cumin

> **Chef's note:** We love rhubarb and have a giant patch at Old Rittenhouse Inn that we make great use of. For winter-weary Northlanders, the rhubarb harvest is a sign that spring has come at last.

## Instructions

Combine all ingredients in a large saucepan and bring to a boil, stirring frequently. Lower heat and cook until mixture is thick (about 10 minutes). This chutney may be served warm or cold as a condiment, or can it in a jar for later use.

# Bayfield Apple Sauce

Yields 2 quarts
Prep/Cook Time: 1 hour 30 minutes

## Ingredients

5 pounds apples (we recommend Wealthy or Macintosh, peeled or unpeeled)
1 cup apple juice or cider
1/3 cup lemon juice
1/4 teaspoon ground nutmeg
1/4 teaspoon ground cinnamon
1/4 teaspoon ground allspice
1-1/2 cups Crab Apple Jelly (see recipe page 161)

## Instructions

Pare, core and quarter the apples. Mix with apple juice, lemon juice and spices in a large stainless steel saucepan. Cook over medium heat until apples are very soft. Remove from heat. Process in a food processor, using a steel blade, until smooth. Add jelly. Process until color is evenly distributed (3-5 seconds).

# Maple-Spiced Squash

Serves 8
Prep/Cook Time: 1 hour 30 minutes

## Ingredients

4 squash (butternut or buttercup)
1/4 cup soft butter
1/2 teaspoon nutmeg or to taste
1/4 teaspoon allspice or to taste
1/4 teaspoon cumin or to taste
1 cup walnuts, chopped
1 cup maple syrup
1/4 cup butter, melted

## Instructions

Preheat oven to 350° F. Cut squash in half and remove the seeds. Cover with foil and bake for 1 hour or until fork tender. Remove from oven, let cool for a few minutes, scoop out pulp and discard the shell.

In an electric mixer fitted with a paddle, combine squash with butter, nutmeg, allspice and cumin. Whip until smooth at medium speed. On low speed, fold in the walnuts, maple syrup and melted butter. Mix until smooth. Remove from mixer. Place in an oiled baking pan or casserole. Return to oven for 10 to 15 minutes and heat until hot throughout before serving.

# Crab Apple Jelly

Yields 6 cups
Prep/Cook Time: Several hours (inactive)

## Ingredients

3 pounds crab apples, fresh, whole, unpeeled
6 cups cold water
1 package pectin (1-3/4 ounces)
6 cups sugar
cheesecloth

## Instructions

Remove stems from crab apples. Place the crab apples in a large stainless steel or non-aluminum kettle and add the water. Bring to a rolling boil, reduce heat and cook until the apples split (about 15 minutes). Line a colander with a double layer of cheesecloth and place it over a large mixing bowl. Pour the contents of the kettle into colander and let juices drip for several hours. This should yield 4 cups of juice. Clean the kettle and return the juice to it. Add pectin and heat until juice begins to boil. Add sugar, stir well. Bring to boil and stir for 75 seconds. Remove from heat and let set for several minutes. Skim off foam. Immediately pour into sterilized jars, seal and process in a water bath according to manufacturer's directions.

# Wassail, Weddings and Special Occasions

## Ceremonially Speaking

It's truly an honor to share in family gatherings and the special moments in peoples' lives, which may be why we specialize in special occasions at Old Rittenhouse Inn.

Sometimes we are simply the hosts of weddings or family reunions. Other times we are the ones who create the events and invite everyone to join us. That is certainly the case with our beloved Wassail Dinner Concerts. And when I say "beloved," I mean by us as much as by the many guests who have visited and made our annual dinners part of their seasonal traditions.

## A-Wassailing We Go

At the Inn, December has meant Wassail Dinner Concerts – our rich tradition of music, hospitality and great food – since 1976.

There are so many memories I associate with this season, starting from my pre-teen years when the Rittenhouse Singers invaded my third-floor bedroom to change into their Victorian costumes before marching through the dining room singing carols to entertain the dinner guests. Eventually I joined that group, under the direction of my father.

Wassail Season is a great way to break up our area's five-month winter, which stretches from the first November snow through those April snowstorms when we start to ask, "Isn't it supposed to be spring?"

As music teachers and musicians, Christmas for Jerry and Mary in Madison always meant a hectic schedule of performances in city concerts and recitals. At the end of their first year of full-time Bayfield living, they felt Christmas here was just too quiet. They decided to bring some music into their house.

They put out a call around town and the voices responded, becoming the first Rittenhouse Chamber Singers. Now, every year when the first leaves turn red, rehearsals begin. In the combined musical voice of the choir are the talents of those who are our

*Don Albrecht*

*Don Albrecht*

*John Noltner*

Jerry directs the Rittenhouse Singers (top) who entertain the dinner guests (left). The dining room really does take on a warm seasonal glow.

neighbors by day. They are lawyers and carpenters, teachers, ministers and a band director. These voices are blended together and put into performance polish under Jerry's direction.

The Singers perform music that accompanies our favorite holiday menus. The Wassail Dinner Concert season begins in early December and continues until Christmas.

Mary and Jerry took a big risk when they traded their promising careers in music education for life in northern Wisconsin.

"Starting in with no formal training in business or cooking isn't a course we'd recommend for anyone," says Mary, "but as we look back, the Inn has provided the perfect opportunity to combine our interests in people, cooking, music, theatre, and historic preservation into a business all our own."

# Weddings & Wonderful Times

Old Rittenhouse Inn has been the site for countless marriage proposals, renewals of vows, wedding ceremonies, anniversaries, birthdays and other family festivities.

Often we already know the families who have been guests for years. Sometimes we are just meeting them during these precious times. Always, their celebrations become part of our lives and remind us of our own special moments.

I particularly love being part of the surprise when people propose marriage. It happens in so many different ways. Once a frequent guest of our Wassail Dinner Concerts wrote a special verse that we inserted into a song. While the Rittenhouse Singers belted out the verse, he got down on his knee with the ring.

Sometimes the gentleman will present an engagement ring in our silver Victorian bread warmer that opens up like a clamshell. He offers "bread" to his special lady and she discovers a sparkling invitation instead. Once a fellow actually wanted the ring hidden inside a mussel shell, making quite an appealing appetizer.

After the proposal (usually) comes the wedding.

As a non-denominational minister, I have performed many wedding services, but I still keenly feel the importance of each event. Perhaps because so many of the ceremonies are done at Le Château, which is where Wendy and I got married, my thoughts turn to our own ceremony.

*Mark Phillips*

164

Wedding couples like these enjoy the grounds outside Le Château (facing page) and the pergola there (top) is a sweet spot for weddings and receptions by the Big Lake. Wendy and I certainly enjoyed the location on our own wedding day (right).

*Erin Larson*

Le Château is perfect for weddings, with its expansive grounds, a pergola and fountain garden, and the large wraparound porch with beautiful Lake Superior views. The pergola is one of our favorite spots, with its beautiful brick foundation and pillars supporting an arbor with grapes growing over it. And, of course, there's the tennis lawn in back of the house – the perfect space for a large tent and an ideal outdoor summer wedding reception. We also offer food and lodging for guests, completing any destination needs.

Wendy and I got married under the pergola, with my father officiating the ceremony and all of our family and friends surrounding us, Lake Superior in magnificent view. I can't imagine a better place to make a lifetime commitment to someone you love.

Another of my favorite memories from our own wedding was the morning of the ceremony. The girls were outside Le Château decorating the pergola with beautiful flowers my dad had picked. I don't know how many lupines there were, but Wendy and her bridesmaids, all smiling and laughing, made a lovely tableau as I spied on them from the third floor, peeking out of the bathroom window. It was a perfect, sunshiny day to get married.

To me this moment signified the "end" of the beginning of our relationship, and the "start" of our new future together. Every time I stand there with a bride and groom, in front of their friends and family, in that beautiful place, that feeling is renewed inside me. When I perform the ceremony, I speak those words from the heart every single time. When I help to start a new future for others, I reflect on our moment there together. It continually reaffirms Wendy's and my marriage.

Of course, we host weddings of all sizes, shapes and colors – from an "elopement" package to weddings with 200 guests – but there is always that nugget of true happiness at the core of every ceremony.

For us, part of the fun is the varied requests. We've done tented weddings with multi-course gourmet catering on the finest china and linens and have also served up a backyard barbecue with grilled chicken, burgers, brats, farmhouse potato salad and all the trimmings.

Inside Le Château, we can serve up to 60 people, plus the space on the porch where many weddings feature a champagne toast. We tend to do at least a couple of winter weddings a year, so season doesn't matter. Love waits for no season, apparently, and we're thrilled to accommodate love whenever it's ripe.

# Sauces

# Champagne Grand Marnier Sauce

Serves 6-8
Prep Time: 10 minutes
Cook Time: 45 minutes

## Ingredients

1 bottle champagne (0.75 liter)
2 bay leaves
10 peppercorns
2 sprigs thyme
2 shallots, rough chopped

2 cups heavy cream
1 Tablespoon chicken base
1/4 cup Grand Marnier

**Chef's tips:** After cream is added, be sure to cook on low for about an hour so cream can reduce and thicken.

This sauce complements a chicken entrée and is great with pasta or as a sauce for veggies.

## Instructions

Combine first five ingredients in a pot and reduce by 75 percent. Add cream and chicken base. Simmer on low for about 60 minutes, then add the Grand Marnier.

# Red Pepper Rouille

Serves 8-10
Prep time: 5 minutes
Cook Time: 5 minutes

## Ingredients

1 cup fresh-roasted red peppers
1/2 teaspoon white pepper
1 teaspoon salt
Pinch cayenne pepper
2 teaspoons white wine vinegar
1 Tablespoon honey
1 teaspoon lemon juice
1/4 cup panko bread crumbs
1/2 cup olive oil

**Chef's tip:** Red Pepper Rouille is great with fried seafood, including the Cumin-spiced Crab Cakes (see recipe page 62) used as a substitute for the mango purée or with the Rittenhouse Quiche (see recipe page 21).

## Instructions

Combine all ingredients in blender except olive oil. Blend until smooth. While blending, carefully pour oil in a slow and steady stream until incorporated.

# Red Wine Caramel Sauce

Serves 8-10
Prep Time: 1 hour
Cook Time: 20 minutes

**Chef's tip:** Red Wine Caramel is a versatile sauce for desserts. Try with poached fruits, custards/brulés, or drizzled over a hot apple crisp. Heaven! Sometimes we use port instead of red wine. Also good with chocolate. You can't go wrong with this one.

## Ingredients

1 bottle dry red wine (0.75 liter), reduced by 85 percent
1/2 cup butter
1 cup and 2 Tablespoons brown sugar
1/2 cup heavy cream
1 teaspoon salt

## Instructions

Heat wine in a saucepan until reduced by 85 percent and set aside. Melt butter in a heavy-bottom saucepan on medium-low heat. Add sugar and salt, stirring occasionally until sugar has melted (about 10 minutes). Add heavy cream and red wine reduction. Keep sauce warm while in use. Cover and store leftovers in refrigerator. It will keep for 10 days or longer.

# Bayfield Raspberry Sauce

Serves 12-14
Prep Time: 5 minutes
Cook Time: 20 minutes

## Ingredients

4 cups fresh raspberries (we suggest Bayfield produce, of course)
1 cup sugar
1/4 cup balsamic vinegar
1 teaspoon salt

## Instructions

Combine all ingredients in a heavy-bottom saucepan and cook on medium-low heat for about 10 minutes. Pour mixture through a sieve and discard solids. For no seeds, use a fine sieve. Transfer sauce to refrigerator to chill.

> **Chef's tip:** We use this sauce extensively with chocolate dishes such as our Flourless Chocolate Torte (see recipe page 180) or even cheesecake. It is also amazing on ice cream with fresh raspberries. Or with empanadas and fried ice cream!

# Sour Cherry Bourbon Sauce

Serves 8-10
Prep Time: 5 minutes
Cook Time: 20 minutes

## Ingredients

2-1/2 cups fresh tart cherries, pitted
1 cup sugar
pinch salt
3 Tablespoons cornstarch
1/4 cup ice water
1/4 cup bourbon

**Chef's tips:** This is a fun sauce because of its versatility. It's equally delicious with sweet or savory dishes. For example, it's great with a dinner entrée, such as seared duck breast, or on breakfast dishes like French toast or waffles with whipped cream. In this book it's paired with a dessert: Panna Cotta (see recipe page 184).

After cooking the cherry mixture with the bourbon, I add another splash of bourbon after sauce is finished.

## Instructions

Combine cherries, sugar and salt in a heavy-bottom saucepan and cook on medium-low heat for about 10 minutes. Mix cornstarch and water in a bowl, then whisk the mixture into cherries to thicken. Stir in bourbon. Serve warm.

# Crème Anglaise

Serves 6-8
Prep Time: 5 minutes
Cook Time: 20 minutes

## Ingredients

1 cup half and half
1 teaspoon vanilla
5 Tablespoons sugar
3 egg yolks
1/4 cup dark rum

## Instructions

In a heavy-bottom saucepan, gently heat the half and half with the vanilla to a simmer. Meanwhile, beat the egg yolks and sugar in mixer for 5 minutes until very foamy. When the half and half is simmering, whip 1/3 of it into the egg foam. Whisk this back into pot and heat, stirring constantly until mixture thickens slightly, but has not scrambled. Remove from heat, add rum and pour through sieve. Chill for 1 hour before serving.

# Marv-elous Christmas Trees

Holiday times mean special seasonal foods and treats, but also other traditions.

For many years, we got our concolor fir trees from Marvin "Marv" Paavola, who passed away in 2009. Marv was a beloved teacher, coach, husband and father here in Bayfield. He always saved his best trees for my parents, and it was always a special day when Marv arrived with the Christmas tree.

Since his passing, I became good friends with his son Tad, who is a fishing buddy of mine and an all-around nice guy. Tad was saving a few concolor firs for us, but they hadn't been big enough until Christmas 2013. Well, they must have had a growth spurt that year because the tree was the biggest we've ever had! It was about 25 feet tall, so we had to trim it down to fit it in the foyer. We were all so excited to have another "Marv" tree.

The beauty of the concolor fir is multifaceted. It grows long needles with a blue-green tint that stay on the tree for months. We've even had it sprout new needles after being set in water.

One year, we put the tree up the week before Thanksgiving, and didn't take it down until after Valentine's Day (it was redecorated with hearts, of course).

The scent of the concolor fir is also amazing: citrusy and fresh. Guests always say it smells like tangerines, grapefruit, mandarin orange or apricot. On the day the tree goes up, and for at least a week afterward, everyone comments about the delightful smell.

It's the perfect backdrop for the twinkling lights and antique ornaments. Many family photos are taken beside it, including our own. ✒

# Saving The Past

## One Courthouse at a Time

Antiques. Architecture. Cooking. History. Music. Volunteerism.

These passions drove my parents in their work and in their personal lives. They were always a little fanatical about preserving treasures of the past, whether antiques or architecture.

No wonder Bayfield is the perfect home for them. The little city retains its historic homes and the flavor of its past. Jerry and Mary got involved with local historic preservation as soon as they purchased the Rittenhouse and spent their first summer in Bayfield. Here they found others who shared their passions and helped dreams become reality.

The old Bayfield County Courthouse would not be standing today but for the efforts of people like my parents, Marjorie Benton and members of the Bayfield Heritage Association. Through will, determination and collective efforts they helped save the courthouse from the wrecking ball.

There is some interesting history behind all of this. In 1886, the county seat was located in Bayfield. The Bayfield County Board of Supervisors hired an expert engineer and surveyor, and charged him with designing a new brownstone courthouse on Washington Avenue. The magnificent late-19th century brownstone was constructed of locally quarried stone with high ceilings, massive staircases and a skylight.

Only six years later, in 1892, the nearby city of Washburn was formed. It was a classic lumber boom town, and with the timber money flowing freely, the population quickly flourished and overtook that of Bayfield. Soon petitions began to circulate, and newspaper ads and flyers appeared urging the county's property owners to change the county seat from Bayfield to Washburn.

The fight was on with serious whining from the Washburnites (the Bayfield take on it) and political shenanigans. For instance, to whip up more votes, plots of land were sold in Washburn for only $1 each, gobbled up by the lumber families and supporting businesses.

Eventually, the numbers won out. In a referendum, the majority of county residents supported the move to Washburn. The Bayfielders tried to block the move with an injunction, but a key official went "missing" for a few days (he turned up in fine health afterwards). During that time, Washburn supporters ransacked the Bayfield Courthouse, stealing all the county records and even taking the furniture.

NPS / Apostle Islands National Lakeshore

The old courthouse still looks good, even without its original clock tower.

Apparently it was easier to ask for forgiveness than permission because the change had already been approved. The county seat was officially moved to Washburn.

Just eight years after the Bayfield Courthouse was built, it sat empty, stripped and abandoned. For the next 80 years, the city of Bayfield struggled with what to do with the frequently vacant building. Finally, city leaders decided to tear it down. Bids for demolition were too expensive so they sold it for next to nothing to Bill McCarty's family. This made the courthouse a good example of what Jerry calls "preservation by neglect" – it cost too much to destroy.

Bill owned a number of historic properties. He didn't have any plans for the courthouse, so he used it as a machine shed and for storage. But by 1976, the McCartys no longer wanted it. They didn't want it torn down, so they worked with Bayfield Heritage

Spencer Robnik

Association to have it restored and remodeled. They offered the building cheap, and the association paid for the work.

Saving the courthouse was a big moment for Mary and Jerry, a high point in their battles to preserve historic buildings. It was the bicentennial year, and I can still see Jerry as auctioneer (did I mention my dad is a Renaissance man?), dressed to the nines with his tall beaver-felt top hat and bow tie standing in front of a tractor trailer all covered in red, white and blue bunting.

It wasn't just Bayfield facing these dilemmas. Many cities around the country went through similar transitions. Mary and Jerry saw this frequently in their travels on the East Coast: Old mansions in gorgeous shore settings destroyed or badly altered. The world had moved on; households didn't include servants to maintain the fussy structures anymore. Nest eggs and trust funds had run dry. The more they saw historic structures elsewhere torn down, the more Mary and Jerry became committed to seeing that Bayfield didn't lose its landmarks.

They developed a pattern of purchasing and repurposing historic buildings: Old Rittenhouse Inn, Le Château, Rittenhouse Cottage, Stark's Grocery Store (the antique shop), Silvernail Guest House, Grey Oak Guest House and the Goldman house. They tried to house businesses in these buildings to sustain them. As Jerry says, one or two old homes in a city can be saved by someone with enough money, but the majority are neglected and end up falling apart.

Bayfield Heritage Association members worked hard to save the courthouse. At the time, they took a lot of flak for saddling the city with a money-losing albatross, but that did not prove to be the case. The courthouse is now headquarters for the Apostle Islands National Lakeshore. Its preservation has made the city richer.

In March 2014, the Bayfield Heritage Association held its 40th anniversary celebration at the historic Bayfield Pavilion on the harbor. In a presentation by Wisconsin Historical Society Director Ellsworth Brown and by association Vice President Marilyn Van Sant, my dad and mom were the inaugural recipients of the "Jerry and Mary Phillips Award for Bayfield Volunteerism" – even the award was named in their honor! It was one of the rare times I've seen my father (nearly) speechless. Jerry insisted at least 50 people in the room were more deserving of the award, and he felt the honor was even greater because of that knowledge.

As I sat with Wendy and the kids that night watching the presentation, I was prouder than ever of all the things my parents have done for our community.

# Desserts

# Poached Pear Crème Brulée

Serves 6
Prep Time: 45 minutes
Cook Time: 1 hour 30 minutes

## Ingredients

3 pears, skin off, halved and cored, we
    prefer Winter or Bartlett pears
3 cups water
1 cup Riesling wine
2 sticks cinnamon
1/2 cup sugar
pinch of salt

## Instructions

Combine all ingredients and bring to boil. Poach pears about 10 minutes until tender,
but still firm. Strain and set aside.

_____

**Brulée Batter**
2 eggs
4 egg yolks
1/3 cup sugar
1 cup heavy cream
1 cup 2% milk
1 vanilla bean, halved and seeded
pinch of salt

6 ceramic dishes (6-inch size)
cake pan large enough to hold the dishes
1/2 cup sugar
1 propane torch

> **Chef's tip:** If you put the cake pan with
> the ceramic dishes into the oven before
> adding the water, you won't risk sloshing
> into the dishes.

1 batch Red Wine Caramel Sauce (see recipe page 169)

Preheat oven to 350° F. Combine first 7 ingredients and whisk well. Pour through
sieve. Place dishes in cake pan and pour batter evenly into dishes. Pour water into
cake pan until level is halfway up dishes. Bake for 30 minutes or until batter is not
jiggly. Let cool for 1 hour. Spoon cooked custard into the cored side of the poached
pears. Sprinkle with sugar and torch to caramelize sugar. Serve with red wine caramel
sauce. For a fun garnish, add whipped cream and berries.

# Figgy Pudding
## with Crème Anglaise

Serves 4-6
Prep Time: 45 minutes
Cook Time: 45 minutes

## Ingredients

1/2 cup butter, softened
1-1/2 cups sugar
1/4 cup canola oil
1/4 cup orange juice concentrate
1/4 cup heavy cream
2 eggs, well beaten
2 cups all-purpose flour, sifted
1/2 teaspoon salt
1 Tablespoon baking powder
1 cup fig paste
1/4 cup dried cranberries
1/4 cup ground, fresh whole orange
1/4 cup Cortland apple, diced
1/4 cup carrot, grated
1 Tablespoon ginger, freshly grated
1 teaspoon ground cinnamon
1/4 teaspoon ground cardamom
1/4 teaspoon ground nutmeg
6 miniature bundt pans
1 hotel pan or large roasting pan
boiling water to fill 2/3 of roasting pan
aluminum foil

*Mark Quiram*

**Chef's tip:** This "piggy" is not the "figgy." We present a paper mâché boar's head during the Wassail Dinner Concerts. Longtime Rittenhouse Singers Ed Kale (left) and Ernie Bliss help out.

## Instructions

Preheat oven to 350° F. Coat bundt pans with nonstick spray. Cream the butter and the sugar. Beat 5 minutes. Add oil, orange juice concentrate, heavy cream, then eggs. Combine well the sifted flour, salt and baking powder, then add the remaining ingredients. Fill bundt pans 3/4 full with batter and place them into the hotel pan. Put pan on oven shelf, then carefully pour boiling water into the pan until 2/3 of bundt pan is covered. Place foil across top of hotel pan, covering everything. Bake for 45 minutes, take foil off and bake an additional 15 minutes. Once removed from oven, let the puddings stand at least 15 minutes in the bundt pans on cooling racks, then gently turn each pan upside down and remove the figgy pudding. Serve warm with Crème Anglaise (see recipe page 172) and fresh whipped cream. Enjoy!

# Flourless Chocolate Torte

Serves 8-12
Prep Time: 45 minutes
Cook Time: 1 hour 45 minutes

# Ingredients & Instructions

### Ganache
1/2 cup heavy cream
2 ounces dark bittersweet chocolate, shaved
2 ounces semi-sweet chocolate chips

In saucepan, bring cream to a simmer. Remove from heat and whisk in chocolate until melted. Set aside.

### Chocolate Torte
1 pound dark bittersweet chocolate, shaved
12 egg whites
1 cup heavy cream
1/2 cup powdered sugar
1 teaspoon vanilla
2 round cake pans (8-inch) plus a rectangular pan large enough to hold both of them
parchment paper
pan spray

Preheat oven to 350° F.

Melt chocolate in a double boiler and transfer it to a mixing bowl. Beat egg whites to soft peak in a second bowl. In third bowl, whip the cream, sugar and vanilla together until cream is stiff. Slowly fold whipped cream mixture into melted chocolate and then fold beaten egg whites into the combined mixture.

Line 2 round cake pans with parchment paper and spray generously. Divide batter evenly between the pans. Place those pans into the larger rectangular pan and place it on an oven shelf. Fill the rectangular pan with water halfway up the round pans. Bake for about 45 minutes or until toothpick inserted into torte comes out clean. Place baked tortes in refrigerator to cool for an hour. Remove from pans and layer top of one torte with ganache. Stack the second torte on top of the first, then spread ganache on top and sides. Set in refrigerator for one hour to set up. Serve with Bayfield Raspberry Sauce (see recipe page 170). You can also do three (or more) thinner layers, as shown here.

# Wisconsin Cheese Pie

Serves 6-8
Prep Time: 15 minutes
Cook Time: 30 minutes

> **Chef's tip:** For a special treat, we serve Wisconsin Cheese Pie topped with apple cider marmalade, slivered apples and whipped cream. Yum, seriously. This was always a big seller when we had an Apple Fest booth.

## Ingredients

1 9-inch pie shell, unbaked
1-1/2 cups cottage cheese or ricotta
16 ounces cream cheese, softened
1-1/2 cups sugar
1 teaspoon vanilla
1 lemon, quartered and seeds removed
4 eggs, slightly beaten
Whipped cream and fresh strawberries for garnish

## Instructions

Preheat oven to 350° F. Combine all ingredients except eggs in food processor, blending until smooth. Fold eggs into the mixture. Pour into pie shell. Bake for 30 minutes. Cool completely before serving. For garnish, we suggest fresh strawberries and whipped cream.

*Paul L. Hayden*

# Black Walnut Bourbon Pie

Serves 10
Prep Time: 15 minutes
Cook Time: 60 minutes

## Ingredients

1 9-inch pie shell, unbaked
3 eggs
1-1/4 cups sugar
1 cup dark corn syrup
1/4 cup bourbon
1/2 cup butter, melted
3/4 cup English walnuts, chopped
1/2 cup black walnuts, chopped
6 ounces semi-sweet chocolate, melted

## Instructions

Preheat oven to 375° F. Beat eggs, sugar and corn syrup. Add bourbon, butter, all the walnuts and chocolate. Pour into pie shell. Bake for 15 minutes. Reduce heat to 325° F and bake until filling is lightly set and crust is golden brown (35-45 minutes). Remove from oven. Cool to room temperature, then refrigerate to complete setting. Serve warm (3-5 minutes in a 325° oven or 20 seconds in a microwave) with vanilla ice cream. This pie is extremely rich and easily serves 10 small slices.

# Vanilla Panna Cotta

Serves 6-8
Prep Time: 15 minutes
Cook Time: 30 minutes
Decorating Time: 20 minutes

**Chef's tip:** After custard is set up, you can either tear off the mold or submerge half of it in warm water to loosen the custard from the mold.

## Ingredients

3 cups heavy cream
1/2 cup sugar
1 vanilla bean, halved and seeded
1 Tablespoon lemon juice
2 Tablespoons ice water
2 envelopes unflavored gelatin (0.25-ounce size)
1 cup sour cream
8 aluminum molds (6-ounce size)

## Instructions

Combine cream, sugar and vanilla bean in 2-quart pot. Turn on medium heat and bring to simmer. Combine gelatin, lemon juice and ice water in a bowl. Stir until gelatin is dissolved. Add to cream mixture once it is to a simmer. Remove from heat and whisk in sour cream. Pull vanilla bean out and pour into molds. Place in refrigerator for at least 2 hours. Peel off the mold (see Chef's tip) and place custard on plate. Serve with Sour Cherry Bourbon Sauce (see recipe page 171).

# Orange Blossom Torte

Serves 10-12
Prep Time: 10 minutes
Cook Time: 30 minutes
Decorating Time: 20 minutes

## Ingredients & Instructions

### Torte
9 eggs, separated
1 cup sugar
1 Tablespoon lemon juice
1-1/2 cups all-purpose flour
2 ounces white chocolate, melted
1/2 cup butter, melted and slightly cooled
orange liqueur to brush, (about 1/2 cup), Grand Marnier is always good

Preheat oven to 325° F. In large mixer bowl, beat egg whites to soft peaks. Gradually add sugar, beating until stiff peaks form. Set aside. Wash beaters. In small mixing bowl fitted with beaters, beat yolks at high speed for 6 minutes or until thick and lemon colored. Add lemon juice. Carefully fold yolk mixture into egg whites. Gradually fold flour into egg mixture. Fold in white chocolate and butter. Pour mixture into two greased 8-inch round baking pans. Bake for 30 minutes or until a toothpick comes out clean. The cake should spring back when gently touched. Invert cakes in pans; allow to cool thoroughly. Loosen cakes; remove from pans. Horizontally slice each layer in half or thirds (as shown) and brush with orange liqueur.

-------------------

### Filling
1/2 cup sour cream
1 8-ounce package cream cheese, softened
1 cup butter, softened
1/4 teaspoon orange peel, grated
1/2 teaspoon orange extract
1 cup powdered sugar

In a medium mixer bowl fitted with paddle, combine sour cream, cream cheese, and butter. Beat until fluffy. Beat in grated orange peel, orange extract and powdered sugar. Place one split cake layer on plate, brush with orange liqueur and then spread about 1/2 cup filling on top. Continue the process, stacking the remaining layers.

## Walnut Vanilla Frosting

1-1/2 cups whipping cream
1 teaspoon vanilla
1/4 teaspoon walnut extract
Orange food coloring
Orange slices and fresh flowers for garnish

**Chef's tip:** You may like to try a buttercream frosting flavored with vanilla, walnut and orange.

Combine whipping cream, vanilla, walnut extract, and a few drops orange food coloring. Whip to stiff peaks. Frost top and sides of the completed cake. If desired, garnish with orange slices and flowers.

# Pot de Crème au Chocolat

Serves 16
Prep Time: 20 minutes
Cook Time: 60 minutes (chilling)

## Ingredients

8 ounces cream cheese, softened
1/2 cup (1 stick) unsalted butter, softened
1/2 cup sour cream
1 cup powdered cocoa
1/2 cup powdered sugar
1/4 cup Kahlua
1/4 cup Amaretto
1/4 cup Grand Marnier
2 teaspoons vanilla
2 drops of almond extract
2 drops of orange extract
4 cups whipping cream, sweetened and stiffly whipped
whipped cream, slivered almonds and shaved chocolate for garnish

## Instructions

Cream the cream cheese, butter and sour cream in a mixer, using paddle on low
speed. Scrape down sides of mixing bowl and beat until the mixture is creamy. Slowly
add the cocoa, sugar, Kahlua, Amaretto, Grand Marnier, vanilla and the extracts,
continuing to mix at low speed. Move the mixture to a different bowl and chill 1 hour.
Just before serving, fold an equal amount of whipped cream into the batter. If you
prefer a more chocolatey, bittersweet pot de crème, use less whipped cream. Serve
topped with whipped cream, slivered almonds and shaved chocolate.

# Banana Hazelnut Cake
## with Chocolate Malt Ice Cream

Serves 4
Prep Time: 15 minutes
Cook Time: 25 minutes, plus overnight chill time for ice cream

# Ingredients & Instructions

### Cake
1/2 pound butter, melted
2 cups bananas, mashed
2 cups powdered sugar
2-1/4 cup all-purpose flour
1 cup hazelnuts,
   toasted and chopped
4 eggs
1 teaspoon baking powder
1/2 teaspoon salt

Preheat oven to 350° F.
Beat all ingredients in a
mixer on high speed until
well combined. Bake until
toothpick comes out clean,
15-25 minutes depending
upon the type of pan used. We use 4 individual, fluted cake pans or use a 9x4x3-inch
bread loaf pan for a single cake.

---

### Chocolate Malt Ice Cream (Philadelphia style)
2 cups cream
1-1/2 cups whole milk
1 cup sugar
3/4 cup malt powder
2 cups semi-sweet chocolate, chips or chopped bar

Heat cream, milk, sugar and malt powder to a boil. Remove from heat and add chocolate,
mixing until melted and smooth. Refrigerate overnight until thoroughly chilled.

Freeze in an ice cream maker following manufacturer's instructions. Place ice cream
in an airtight container and put it in the freezer. For best results, be sure ice cream is
frozen overnight before serving.

# Rum Baba with Poached Apples

The Rum Baba is a very popular Eastern European bread-like item, here turned into an elegant, and warming, fall dessert featuring Bayfield apples.

Serves 6
Prep Time: 60 minutes
Cook Time: 60 minutes

## Ingredients & Instructions

1 packet active dry yeast (or 2-1/4 teaspoons)
2 Tablespoons warm whole milk
1/2 Tablespoon sugar
1 teaspoon salt
1-1/8 cups bread flour
3 eggs
5 Tablespoons butter, cubed

In mixing bowl, proof the yeast in warm milk for 10 minutes. Add sugar, salt and flour, mixing on low. Add eggs and mix with dough hook for about 5 minutes or until a smooth dough forms. Cover and allow to rise for one hour or until doubled. Meanwhile, cube butter and allow to soften at room temperature.

When dough has doubled, add butter one chunk at a time with mixer running on medium speed with dough hook. This will take a while. Continue mixing until the dough is satiny smooth. Remove dough from bowl and cut into 6 portions. Form into balls and place in greased brioche molds or other small, individual baking tins. Allow to rise until doubled (about 20-30 minutes) and bake in preheated 400° F oven for 15-20 minutes or until golden brown. Remove from tins and allow to cool.

_____

**Rum Baba "Dunk"**
1 cup water
1/2 cup sugar
1 cinnamon stick
1 orange, juice and peel
1/2 cup dark rum or to taste

Simmer water, sugar, cinnamon and orange juice and peel for 10 minutes. Add rum and cool to room temperature.

## Apple Garnish

6 medium-sized crisp, tart apples (we like Honey Crisp, Jonafree,
   Cortland or Liberty)
1 vanilla bean, split and seeded
1 quart water
2 cups sugar

Core the apples and cut in wedges, but do not peel. Bring water and sugar to a boil and
add split vanilla bean and seeds. Add apples and simmer until just tender, 5-8 minutes.

_____

## Mulled Cider Reduction

1 quart apple cider
ground mulling spices

Bring cider and spices to a boil in non-reactive pan and reduce by about a factor
of 6 or until almost syrupy. Occasionally skim the froth off the top, keeping an eye
that it does not reduce down too far and burn. Allow to cool. The reduced cider
will keep, covered, in the refrigerator almost indefinitely.

## To Finish

Immerse each baba in the rum "dunk" for about 30 seconds to saturate. Serve with
a 1/2 ounce or so of the mulled cider reduction drizzled over each and garnish with
the apple wedges and plenty of whipped cream.

*Gregg Thompson*

# Truly Happy Hours

## My Aunt Julie

For many of our guests, my aunt, Julie Phillips, is the face of the Old Rittenhouse Inn and certainly of the Landmark Restaurant. She often serves their breakfast, then welcomes them in the evening for dinner. She's also an amazing cook and baker (best baking-powder biscuits ever) and these days Aunt Julie can also turn out a mighty fine cocktail.

Aunt Julie, Dad's youngest sister in a family of 10, first came to Bayfield in the summer with her parents, my grandpa and grandma, who rented a house a few blocks from the Inn. Julie started work at the Inn before going to college, spent summers here while attending college, and moved to Bayfield and stayed after she graduated.

Julie loves Christmas. She embodies the spirit of the season at our Wassail Concerts and at our annual family gatherings. She seems to have a gift for everyone and every gift includes handmade chocolates, bows, ribbons and decorations. Her packages look perfect, as if done by an elf in Santa's workshop. But Julie's real gift is her smile and warm personality, the love and care with which she goes about her daily tasks.

I have my own story that shows Aunt Julie's generosity. As a youngster on my way home after fishing, I once met Julie carrying a fresh bouquet of wildflowers. She asked if I was going to Grandma June's house. "Yes," I said.

Julie, running late for work, asked me to bring Gram the bouquet, so I took the flowers.

When Grandma June opened the door and saw those flowers, her face lit up. She gave me a giant hug. "The flowers are so beautiful! Did you pick them?"

"Yes!" I blurted out, unable in the light of those twinkling eyes to admit that I had not picked them myself.

A day or two later, Julie cornered me in private. "Did you tell June that you picked those flowers?"

Ashamed, I hung my head, nodding.

"Well, I didn't tell her it wasn't you who picked them," Julie said, "but you and I both know it's not true. It's important to tell the truth."

Julie values truth, honesty and fairness. I value Julie. She's the best aunt a person could wish for, plus an exemplary innkeeper. I would do anything for her … and not just because of her gentle corrections and because she can keep an embarrassing secret.

Because so many guests know Aunt Julie and because she is the natural one to introduce our "Cocktail Hour" recipes, I've asked her to say a few word about the Inn …

# Musings from Our Mixologist

I came to work at Old Rittenhouse Inn in early May 1981. The Inn was going strong, and Mary and Jerry had gotten much too busy for their original "Ma and Pa" approach. They needed help.

I started in the kitchen, with Mary as my teacher. I loved to cook and had done so for my family ever since I could reach the stovetop. I worked as Mary's sous chef, prepping for the day's meals. Long ago I lost track of how many chicken breasts I stuffed, En Croute de la Mer I assembled or pork chops I seasoned, seared and braised. We ran full-steam, seven days a week, three meals a day. I loved every minute.

After several years, Mary decided that my true talents were wasted in the kitchen. Being an outgoing person, I should be out on the floor, Mary believed, waiting tables and reciting the menu aloud as Jerry did. My new job back then delighted me … and still does.

There's something exceptional about *telling* guests the menu rather than just having them read it. For me, it's like being on stage, with the guests as my audience. It's theater and storytelling, so the delivery is as important as what is said. And like any play, there's a certain amount of rehearsing and remembering lines. It's second nature to me now, so I just need a few moments to myself before the evening starts to get into the proper frame of mind and to choose the words to describe our new menu items. I long ago memorized our signature dishes and favorite entrées, so only the evening specials require a new repertoire – and I may not know until I arrive if the chef makes a last minute change.

Happily, I know our food and service will impress, so it's with a lot of confidence I go to a table to describe the night's menu. Often, our guests' appreciation of the meal starts with the lush descriptions. I know I'm on track when I start to hear the ooohs and aaahs. (Of course we do have printed menus available for those who like to ponder their options on the page.)

Describing your dinner is only one of my roles here, though. My newest job involves a different kind of creativity.

When I came to work for Mary and Jerry, I knew nothing about wine. Mom's "hot toddy" – mostly hot water, sugar and a splash from the "medicinal" jug of Mogan David Concord grape wine kept under the sink – was the only wine I'd tasted. So my education in fine wines began at Old Rittenhouse Inn. Soon I became interested in all wines, reds to blushes to whites. When I started, first Mary and then our maître d', David Saetre, who knew a great deal about wines, did all the wine ordering. I worked under David, learning more, and when he left on a different career path, I became the wine/beverage manager.

Over the years, I expanded my repertoire to include bartending and custom cocktails. I love creating new things and so started to invent fresh new cocktails. For several years, we offered a tropical drink-themed special event during our quiet season. That gave me the perfect opportunity to try out my concoctions, such as the Guava Colada, Shark Bite, Lava Flow and Spotted Lizard Margarita. I've acquired a large, ever-expanding folder of recipes.

In 2011, *Imbibe Magazine* asked me to submit a cocktail recipe. They wanted a hot cider. I had the perfect one, the Rittenhouse Wassail Punch, and sent it off to them. It was featured on their website, and then included in their first-ever hardcover book, *The American Cocktail*.

Aunt Julie mixing up Wassail Punch.

In 2013, I entered a contest sponsored by the Scottish whisky company Bruichladdich. They had just come out with their small-batch gin, The Botanist: Artisan Islay Dry Gin, and they were looking for recipes. I entered my Lake Superior Clear Water Bloody Mary recipe and it was one of the winners.

Over the years, I've done many jobs at the Inn – dishwashing, housekeeping, prep chef, waitress, maître d', front desk receptionist, floor staff manager, wine/beverage manager and mixologist. I've enjoyed all of the jobs, and each day, I try to make what I do count.

Mary and Jerry started a wonderful B&B, and now I'm so happy to see Mark and Wendy taking great care to run it well. My goal is to make every guest who stays with us enjoy Old Rittenhouse Inn as much as I do.

# Cocktails

# Red Raspberry Cordial

This is a special treat that is very simple to make – all it takes is time. The recipe originates from my parents' friends, John and Jean Haveman. As a child, I remember my mother making this and storing it down in the wine cellar. I loved the rows of glass gallon jars filled with berries, sugar and alcohol. As the days and seasons passed, the color faded from the berries while the liquid surrounding them turned deeper shades of ruby red.

We occasionally present this cordial during the dessert course as a treat for couples celebrating honeymoons, anniversaries and other special occasions.

Serves 4
Prep time: 10 minutes
Cook Time: 30 minutes
Wait Time: 4-36 months

## Ingredients

1 quart raspberries
2 cups sugar
1 bottle gin (750 ml)

> **Julie's tip:** Pick your choice of gin, but remember: The better the gin, the better the cordial. Bombay is always good.

## Instructions

Put all ingredients together in covered glass jar. Stir until sugar is dissolved into the gin. Store in a dark place and shake several times per week. The cordial is ready to go after about 4 months, but will keep for much longer. When ready to serve, open jars and strain through a cheesecloth. Bottle and enjoy during your special occasions.

*Erin Larson*

# Crimson Jul

This is a custom cocktail created for the holiday season by our mixologist Julie Phillips. It was featured in the December/January 2013 issue of *Lake Superior Magazine*.

Serves 2-3

## Ingredients

11 sprigs fresh mint
1 Tablespoon fresh ginger root, grated
2 ounces dark rum
2-1/2 ounces vanilla rum
4 ounces Cranberry Purée (see recipe below)
1 ounce simple syrup (see below)
1 ounce fresh orange essence (see below)
1 ounce fresh lime juice
sliced fresh cranberry
2 orange twists

> **Julie's tip:** I've found out one essential part of creating a good drink is to start with fresh ingredients. It takes a little longer to make the drinks, but the results are well worth the extra time. When preparing a drink I usually make enough of the special ingredients so that I can refrigerate the extra and make more drinks quickly later.

## Instructions

Muddle mint and ginger in shaker. Add the remaining ingredients and shake with ice. Strain into a cocktail glass. Garnish with sliced fresh cranberries and orange twist.

---

**Julie's Cranberry Purée**
2 bags fresh cranberries (12-ounce size)
1-1/2 cups cranberry juice

**Simple Syrup**
water (1 part)
sugar (2 parts)

**Orange Essence**
2 navel oranges, peels and all

To make fresh cranberry purée, start with fresh cranberries, rinsed and sorted. Add cranberry juice and cook to boiling, turn burner down to simmer and cook for 10 minutes or until berries have popped. Strain this through a fine mesh strainer. Use the back of a spoon to push the purée through the screen. This purée adds a wonderful silky texture to the drink.

While the cranberries are cooking, make the simple syrup by cooking 1 part water to 2 parts sugar. Bring this to a boil until sugar is dissolved. Let this mixture cool.

For the orange essence, use a juicer to process 2 whole navel oranges, including peels.

# Julie's Margarita

Serves 6

This is Julie's tried and true recipe for a homemade margarita. This doesn't taste like the pre-fab mixer margaritas; it's a blast of fresh, vibrant citrus with a smoky hit from the tequila. We serve this in a chilled glass with a salt rim. Personally, I like it best with a guajillo pepper salt rim for a spicy bite that picks up the smoky notes of the tequila.

## Ingredients

1-1/2 cups tequila
3/4 cup triple sec
1/2 cup fresh lemon juice
1/2 cup fresh lime juice
splash of fresh orange juice
1 cup sugar
3-3/4 cups water

**Julie's tip:** To make Raspberry or Strawberry Margaritas, make the above recipe and blend in 2 pints of fresh berries. If you want it to be seedless, run the mixture through the blender and then through a fine mesh strainer.

## Instructions

Stir all ingredients together until sugar dissolves and serve over ice. For a blended margarita, blend mixture with 3 cups of ice.

# Perfect Piña Colada

Serves 1-2

I am a sucker for Piña Coladas. They are my kryptonite, my secret weakness. Wendy and I once stayed at a resort in Jamaica with a poolside bar that served yummy blender drinks in tiny little glasses. Despite the hefty price, we couldn't stop ordering them because they were so delicious. This recipe always makes me think of that trip.

## Ingredients

2 ounces cream of coconut
3 ounces white rum
4 ounces pineapple juice
1 ounce pineapple, crushed
2 cups of ice
splash of cherry juice for garnish

**Julie's tip:** Try topping it off with a splash of Amaretto.

## Instructions

Blend ingredients in blender until smooth. Pour into chilled glasses and garnish with a splash of cherry juice.

# Lake Superior
# Clear Water Bloody Mary

Serves 6

The secret to this drink is tomato water. This faintly rose-colored liquid may not look terribly impressive at first glance, but its flavor is the very essence of tomato. This cocktail is ultra-refreshing on hot summer days. Make it by the pitcher and watch it disappear like a ship in the mist.

# Ingredients & Instructions

4 pounds tomatoes, chopped
1/2 pound English or Persian hothouse cucumber, skin on, chopped
1 celery stalk, with leaves removed, chopped
3 sprigs lemon thyme
kosher salt (for recipe and for the glass rim)
juice from half a lemon
2 squares cheesecloth (18 inches each)
9 ounces Botanist gin (or your favorite)
lemon slices
6 cocktail-style bamboo skewers
fresh mozzarella pearls
1-inch pieces of your favorite snack stick sausages
cherry tomatoes
blue cheese stuffed olives
2 dried guajillo chiles

---

## Tomato Water

Purée the tomatoes, hothouse cucumbers, celery stalk, lemon thyme and lemon juice in a blender until smooth. In a large bowl, strain the mixture through a cheesecloth-lined, fine-mesh sieve. Let drain, without stirring, until 3 cups of liquid are collected (about 2 hours). Discard solids left in strainer. Season with kosher salt to taste. This part of the cocktail can be prepared in advance, and may be stored covered in the refrigerator for up to 4 days.

---

## Chile-Salt Mix

Put 2 dried guajillo chiles in a spice grinder and blend them into fine powder. (I use a small coffee mill.) Mix 1 part ground chile to 2 parts coarse kosher salt on a small plate.

---

## To Finish

Run a lemon wedge around the rim of 6 tall glasses and dip them into the guajillo chile-salt mixture. Fill each glass with ice. Add 1-1/2 ounces of Botanist gin (or your favorite) to each glass. Fill with tomato water and stir.

We like to garnish with skewers that alternate cherry tomatoes, mozzarella pearls and blue cheese-stuffed olives and finish with a piece of sausage. Or add a fresh summer touch as in this photo with celery and asparagus stalks. Add a long, slim straw and a lemon slice to each glass. Enjoy!

# Santa Baby Cosmo

Serves 2

**Julie's tip:** Try different flavored Zygo vodkas for variety.

## Ingredients

2 ounces Zygo vodka
1 ounce cranberry purée (see Julie's recipe page 197)
1 ounce fresh lime juice
1 ounce simple syrup
1 ounce Grand Marnier
splash of sparkling wine or champagne
sliced cranberries and wedge of orange to garnish

## Instructions

Mix the first five ingredients in a shaker of ice and pour into martini glasses. Top with a splash of sparkling wine/champagne. Garnish with a wedge of orange and sliced cranberries.

# Rittenhouse Wassail Punch

Serves 10-12

## Ingredients

12 whole cloves
6 whole allspice
12 whole white peppercorns
3 sticks cinnamon
1/2-inch fresh ginger root, peeled and sliced
1 gallon fresh apple cider
6 ounces cranberry juice
3/4 cup light brown sugar, packed
1 ounce (per cup) bourbon. Use good quality; my preference is Knob Creek.
1 whole nutmeg for garnish
cinnamon sticks for garnish

## Instructions

Wrap the cloves, allspice, peppercorns, cinnamon sticks and ginger root in cheesecloth and tie with kitchen string. In a large pot, heat the apple cider, cranberry juice, brown sugar and spice bag. Bring to a boil, reduce heat and simmer 30 minutes.

For serving, add bourbon to a mug and fill with the punch. Grate fresh nutmeg on the top and add a cinnamon stick. The punch can be refrigerated for several days in a covered container. If you like lots of spice flavors, make this the day before and leave the spice bag in the container overnight in the refrigerator. When you're ready, just heat and serve.

# Serendipitous Appletini

This is a variation on the Wassail punch recipe on the preceding page.

Serves up to 6

## Ingredients & Instructions

### Spiced Cider Basic Recipe
1 gallon fresh apple cider
6 ounces cranberry juice
3/4 cup light brown sugar, packed
6 whole allspice
12 whole cloves
12 whole white peppercorns
3 sticks cinnamon
1/2-inch fresh ginger root, peeled and sliced

Wrap the cloves, allspice, ginger and cinnamon sticks in cheesecloth and tie with kitchen string. In a large pot, heat the apple cider, cranberry juice, brown sugar and spice bag. Bring to a boil, reduce heat to medium high and continue to boil for about 30 minutes. Remove half and cool the cider, placing it into the refrigerator to chill. For the Apple Cider Reduction Syrup, continue with the remaining half as below.

---

### Apple Cider Reduction Syrup
Keep ingredients boiling on medium for another 30 minutes and take out spice packet, then continue to boil until it reduces down to a syrupy consistency, about 30-40 minutes. Once you have the syrup made for the garnish you can keep it for a month in the refrigerator. You will need to warm it up to room temperature before you will be able to use it for the drink.

---

### Cocktail

1 ounce Apple Cider Reduction Syrup
12 ounces chilled Spiced Cider Basic Recipe
4 ounces Canadian whisky
1 ounce New Glarus Serendipity (fruited sour ale)
Thin-sliced apples

Garnish two 10-ounce martini glasses with the Apple Cider Reduction Syrup. You can get creative and swirl this all around the inside of the glass (see photo) and half of the rim so that you get the flavor of the reduction. For each martini, put 6 ounces of the chilled spiced cider and 2 ounces Canadian whisky in an ice-filled metal cocktail shaker. Shake vigorously until ice begins to form on the outside of the metal shaker. Pour into the prepared cocktail glass.

Garnish with sliced apple and top with the splash of New Glarus Serendipity.

# A Last Word or Two

Thank you for joining me at the table, to read the history of this Inn and our family of relatives, staff and guests. I hope you will sample the bounty of our recipes contained within, and share them with your own family and friends.

I've been blessed to grow up B&B, and to have the benefit of the many celebrations and friends we've made here at Old Rittenhouse Inn. I wouldn't trade it for anything.

Now that I'm doing the job of innkeeper and parent, just as my folks did, I see the larger picture. On some level, everything that Mom and Dad, and Wendy and I do at the Inn is for our children and future generations. We're not just building a business, but also a family legacy to which our children (and our guests' children) can always return if they choose.

Ultimately, these old buildings will transcend our time here. They were here before us, and God willing, they'll be here long after us. I often tell guests this, and it's the truth: We are not so much the owners of these properties as we are the stewards.

During our time here, our job is to protect and preserve these buildings so that future generations may enjoy them. We hope some of those future generations come from a long line of Phillips. And we hope your families – your future generations – will still be coming to stay with us.

*Cathy Schmidt*
Le Château is front and center in an autumn waterfront view of Bayfield with the retired U.S. Coast Guard cutter *Sundew*, now privately owned, visiting beside the breakwater.

# INDEX

## PEOPLE & PLACES

# From Lake Superior Port Cities Inc.
## Since 1979

**Lake Superior Magazine**
A bimonthly, regional publication covering the shores along Michigan, Minnesota, Wisconsin and Ontario

**Lake Superior Travel Guide**
An annually updated mile-by-mile guide

**Lake Superior, The Ultimate Guide to the Region, Third Edition**
Softcover: ISBN 978-1-938229-17-6

Hugh E. Bishop:
**The Night the Fitz Went Down**
Softcover: ISBN 978-0-942235-37-1

**By Water and Rail: A History of Lake County, Minnesota**
Hardcover: ISBN 978-0-942235-48-7
Softcover: ISBN 978-0-942235-42-5

**Haunted Lake Superior**
Softcover: ISBN 978-0-942235-55-5

**Haunted Minnesota**
Softcover: ISBN 978-0-942235-71-5

Beryl Singleton Bissell:
**A View of the Lake**
Softcover: ISBN 978-0-942235-74-6

Bonnie Dahl:
**Bonnie Dahl's Superior Way, Fourth Edition: A Crusing Guide to Lake Superior**
Softcover: ISBN 978-0-942235-92-0

Joy Morgan Dey, Nikki Johnson:
**Agate: What Good Is a Moose?**
Hardcover: ISBN 978-0-942235-73-9

Daniel R. Fountain:
**Michigan Gold & Silver, Mining in the Upper Peninsula**
Softcover: ISBN 978-1-938229-16-9

Chuck Frederick:
**Spirit of the Lights**
Softcover: ISBN 978-0-942235-11-1

Marvin G. Lamppa:
**Minnesota's Iron Country**
Softcover: ISBN 978-0-942235-56-2

Daniel Lenihan:
**Shipwrecks of Isle Royale National Park**
Softcover: ISBN 978-0-942235-18-0

Betty Lessard:
**Betty's Pies Favorite Recipes**
Softcover: ISBN 978-0-942235-50-0

Mike Link & Kate Crowley:
**Going Full Circle: A 1,555-mile Walk Around the World's Largest Lake**
Softcover: ISBN 978-0-942235-23-4

James R. Marshall:
**Shipwrecks of Lake Superior, Second Edition**
Softcover: ISBN 978-0-942235-67-8

**Lake Superior Journal: Views from the Bridge**
Softcover: ISBN 978-0-942235-40-1

Mark Phillips:
**The Old Rittenhouse Inn Cookbook: Meals & Memories from the Historic Bayfield B&B**
Softcover: ISBN 978-1-938229-19-0

Kathy Rice:
**The Pie Place Café Cookbook: Food & Stories Seasoned by the North Shore**
Softcover: ISBN 978-1-938229-04-6

Howard Sivertson:
**Driftwood: Stories Picked Up Along the Shore**
Hardcover: ISBN 978-0-942235-91-3

**Schooners, Skiffs & Steamships: Stories along Lake Superior's Water Trails**
Hardcover: ISBN 978-0-942235-51-7

**Tales of the Old North Shore**
Hardcover: ISBN 978-0-942235-29-6

**The Illustrated Voyageur**
Hardcover: ISBN 978-0-942235-43-2

**Once Upon an Isle: The Story of Fishing Families on Isle Royale**
Hardcover: ISBN 978-0-962436-93-2

Frederick Stonehouse:
**Wreck Ashore: United States Life-Saving Service, Legendary Heroes of the Great Lakes**
Softcover: ISBN 978-0-942235-58-6

**Shipwreck of the Mesquite**
Softcover: ISBN 978-0-942235-10-4

**Haunted Lakes** (the original)
Softcover: ISBN 978-0-942235-30-2

**Haunted Lakes II**
Softcover: ISBN 978-0-942235-39-5

**Haunted Lake Michigan**
Softcover: ISBN 978-0-942235-72-2

**Haunted Lake Huron**
Softcover: ISBN 978-0-942235-79-1

Julius F. Wolff Jr.:
**Julius F. Wolff Jr.'s Lake Superior Shipwrecks**
Hardcover: ISBN 978-0-942235-02-9
Softcover: ISBN 978-0-942235-01-2

www.LakeSuperior.com
1-888-BIG LAKE (888-244-5253)
Outlet Store: 310 E. Superior St., Duluth, MN 55802